Stamberg

berg

Aferi

at

RIZZOLI
NEW YORK

First published in the United States of America in 1997
by Rizzoli International Publications, Inc.
300 Park Avenue South, New York NY 10010

Copyright © 1997 by Rizzoli International Publications, Inc.
Foreword © Joseph Rosa
Introduction © Paul Goldberger

Library of Congress Cataloging-in-Publication Data
Stamberg Aferiat architecture / introduction by Paul Goldberger ;
foreword by Joseph Rosa ; contributions by Charles Gwathmey,
David Hockney, and Richard Meier.
      p.   cm.
Includes bibliographical references.
ISBN 0–8478–2011–4 (pb)
1. Stamberg Aferiat Architecture (Firm)
2. Color in architecture—United States.
3. Texture in architecture—United States.
4. Space (Architecture)—United States.
I. Gwathmey, Charles, 1938-   II. Hockney, David.
III. Meier, Richard, 1934-
NA737.S628S72   1997   96-47014
720' .92'273—DC21   CIP

Designed by Bureau (NY)
Printed and bound in Singapore

contents

Built

Projects

To me every hour of the light and dark is a miracle,
Every cubic inch of space is a miracle...
—Walt Whitman

The spirits of lost friends live on
within us all. The insights and delight
they brought to the world inhabit
our hearts and minds. These bequests
are our guides.

This book is dedicated
to five of the closest friends
we have ever had—
Christopher Mann,
Bill Miller and Gary Reynolds,
Nathan Kolodner and
Rene Amrein—as well as
too many other friends,
all lost to AIDS.

Ack nowl edg me nts

Among the many truisms spoken by Philip Johnson, none is truer than that architecture is a social art. Our projects would not have come to pass or been what they are without the involvement of many people. We do, indeed, owe the proverbial *mille grazie*.

With great love and affection, our thanks go out to five people who took the amazing leap from being friends or family members to being clients—and remained both. Their faith in us is the greatest of treasures. Thank you Jill and Al Jarnow. Thank you Jill and Peter Kraus. Thank you Liz Needle.

We hope that the following pages have borne out the convictions of David Morton, Senior Editor at Rizzoli, that this book should be. Our thanks to him for conceiving the book and carrying it through with such wisdom and elegance. Certainly his decision to pursue a book on our work is based, in large measure, on the unfailingly exquisite and insightful photographs by Paul Warchol. Inspired by Richard Meier's consistency in commissioning Ezra Stoller to photograph all of his early work until Stoller's retirement, we have made a "lifetime contract" with Paul Warchol. And just as Paul Warchol's photographs have helped us see our work anew, so have Joseph Rosa's words. His perceptions and historical perspective have become an integral part of our design ideology. That Paul Goldberger, whose writings on architecture have given us so much, has been such a great champion of our work is more than we should hope for. How can we thank him enough for his essay? That three artists whose works serve so much as our artistic compass have written essays on our own work is the greatest of honors. Thank you Richard Meier, Charles Gwathmey, and David Hockney.

Thanks to the other people whose lives have touched ours and have most guided us artistically:
Marcel Breuer, Lewis Davis, Dino Gavina, Henry Geldzahler, Charles Jencks, Man Ray, Robert Siegel, and Michael Webb. Thanks to Frank Israel for his friendship, artistic lead, and codification of the concept of "clients and their shadows."

Thanks to our clients—so many of whom have become great friends— for commissioning work, putting trust in us, and recommending us to their friends:
The Bartholomew Consolidated School Corporation/Ray Ziegler, President; Jay Chiat and Donatella Brun, Steve Burison, Riki Conway; the Cummins Engine Foundation/William I. Miller; Jorge Fisher Jr., Ivory and Jack Freidus, Susan Halpern, Richard Hamburger, Naomi and Stu Hample, Anita Hoffman, Robert F. and Lynn Johnson, Louis Bradbury and Douglas Jones, Edward Shumsky and Susan Kronick, Stuart Uram and Lillian Langotsky, Jeanette Lerman; the Board of Directors of The Long Island Children's Museum/Lisa Greene, President; Jeffrey Loria, Carl Magnusson, Ed McCabe, Nazir and Rabia Mir, Nancy Wexler and Herb Pardes, Tom and Linda Platt, Myron and Peggy Polenberg and the late Noel Nelson Polenberg, Steve Nelson and Shirley Sarna, Bobby Short, Ricki Lake and Rob Sussman; Wright Line/Bill Housh, President. Very special thanks go to Judy Habib, an early and still great champion; to Bill Persky and Joanna Patton, Lucy and Phil Suarez, and Marsha Pinkstaff, for their very compelling words in promoting us to prospective clients, enabling our practice to move forward.

Thanks to the people in our office, whose contributions to the projects they have worked on have been immeasurable:
Kimberly Ackert, Catherine Bogard, Kathleen Byrne, Kevin Estrada, Blake Goble, Jamie Meunier, Robin Noble, Michael Regan, Glen Rescalvo, Paola Sanguinetti Rivas, John Schneider, and Lawrence Zeroth.

Thanks to the contractors who have built our designs, and to the people who worked on the construction:
Lou Balistrieri, Joseph Chasas, John Depp Glass, Ray Finelli Construction, Bohn Fiore Inc., Portia Munson and Jared Handelsman, Ted Kohl, David Meves Construction, Bob and Brian Pear, Tom and John Sama, Hank Schott, Scorcia & Diana, Sheehan and Scott Construction, Nick Sutera, and Wildes Construction.

Thanks to the consultants who have made sure everything is just right:
Robert Anderson of Jam Consultants, Sanford Berger, Jordan Fox, Glen Fries, Richard Gold, Frank Radics and Jim Heitmann, Tim Hunter and Steven Donaghey, Jerry Kugler, Ed Messina of Severud Associates, Tim Moyers, Don Friedman, Nat Oppenheimer, and Robert Silman.

Thanks to the people who have helped to make sure that our projects were wonderfully published:

Stanley Abercrombie, Juliana Balint, Marilyn Bethany, Gilda Bojardi, Elizabeth Sverbeyeff Byron, Dennis Cahill, Deborah Dietsch, John Morris Dixon, Anne Foxley, Vera Graaf, Paula Rice Jackson, Sarah Kaltman Cantor, Andrea Loukin, Judith Nasatir, Victoria Newhouse, Giovanni Odoni, Joseph Giovannini and Christine Pittel, Paul Ryan, Durston Saylor, Suzanne Slesin, Suzanne Stephens, Ellen Stern, Verne, and Pilar Viladas. Constant thanks to Jonas Damon in Paul Warchol's office; to Megan McFarland at Rizzoli, who has helped to make this journey as wonderful as the destination; to Tom Hooper for the remarkable model photographs; to Mario Carrieri for the inspired furniture photographs; to Ezra and Erica Stoller for the photographs of Richard Meier's buildings; and to Donald Moffett, Marlene McCarty, and Claudia Brandenburg of Bureau(NY), who have made the journey and the destination equally beautiful. There is not quite enough we can say to thank Therese Bissell, Louis Oliver Gropp, Wendy Lyon Moonan, Mayer Rus, and Beverly Russell.

Thanks to our favorite people at our favorite design and art resources who have, sometimes miraculously, made sure things arrived perfectly and quickly:

Jonathan Adler, Michael Anchin, Ray Barbosa, Jeffrey Bonin (Donghia), George and Louise Beylerian, Bill Costa (Flos & Luceplan), Karen Stoller, Barbara Delano, and Ken and Marabeth Tyler (Tyler Graphics), Loretta Howard, Louise Eliasor, and Andre Emmerich (Andre Emmerich Gallery), Vernon Evenson (FCI), Elizabeth Goldfeder and Eric Kahan, Robert Homma, Erick Johnson (Akari Associates), David Keats (Rosecore), Arthur Liebowitz, William Lipton, Charlene Loo (EverReady), Massimo Lucarini (Boffi), Julia MacFarlane (Manhattan Ad Hoc), Sixta Minaya (Palazzetti), Robert Mongiardini, Audrey Parker (A.R.P. Interiors), Russ Roberts (Art Services), Piera Rimaldi and Mira Mio (B&B), Dennis Miller, Eric Norup, Loren Pack (ABC Carpet and Home), Tom Radko, Bruce Tomb (IOOA), Deborah Rathbun (ICF), Nancy Reedy (Cassina/Flos), Yancey Richardson, Sergio and Monique Savarese (Dialogica), Godley-Schwan, and Dorothy Wako (Beautiful Flowers).

And thanks are never enough to our families, who have been so supportive:

Bee, Herb, and Winifred Aboff; Stuart and Barbara Aferiat, Daniel and Carol Aferiat, Geraldine Aferiat, Collette Isakoff, and Miriam and Walter Ress. And thanks to Bernice Samelson, our "fifth business." And with love to our parents, Lois and Mel Stamberg and, in memoriam, Charlotte and Albert Aferiat.

Thanks to our huge network of friends, who have shared both trials and joys; given us support, encouragement, and counsel; and helped us find clients. Some have helped in small ways, and some in very big ways:

Jacob and Constance Alspector, Travis Anderson, Brian Baggot, Tina Ball, Jeffrey Banks, Charles Klein and Daniel Baudendistal, Mario Bellini, Keith Berg, Sandy and Michele Berger; Celia, George, and Albert Birtwell; Marc Blackwell, Williard Spiegelman and Kenneth Bleeth, Todd Blumenthal, Terrence McNally and Gary Bonasorte, Susan Bond, Marlyn Brill, Jeanette Brown, Nick and Cary Browse, The Amrein/Brunner Family, Ed Baynard and Dietmar Busse, Mischa and Chloe Byruck, Sarah and Marcus Byruck, Toshiko Mori and Jamie Carpenter, Peter Cervi, Julienne Christensen, Katherine Helmond and David Christian, David Christmas, Al Pfeiffer, Mat Clum, Peter Cohen, Barrie and Lisa Conway, Robert McDonald and Robert Corey, Mario Corradi, Mark Cox, Ian and Abby Crofts, Nicole DeGalea, Ann and Pier Del Pero, Keith Rothman and Frankie Diago, Alain de Puymorin and Gerard Di Giacomo, Andrea Dobbis, Benjamin Doller, Eric DuFour, Gregory Evans, Ian Falconer, Jim Farah, Alexandra Feldon, Jon Nathanson and Richard Feldman, Barbara Abrams and Roy Feldman, Joni Weyl and Sidney Felsen, Robin Thomashauer and David Florin, Steven Forman, Lois Freedman, Amory Houghton and Stephanie French, Rina Gerevitz, Rick and Randy Globus, Dorothy and Steve Globus, Gil and Rhoda Graham, Ann Upton and David Graves, Lisa Green, Gerald and Evelyn Gurland, Bette Ann Gwathmey, Marc Hacker, Betsy Jablow and Robin Hall, Sherri Hodes, Tom Huser, Ira Frazen and Stephen Jacobs, Margot Jacqz, Scott Kemper, Jean Koefoed, Arthur Lambert, Aaron McDonald and Sarah Landis, Ron Bentley and Sal La Rosa, Ginette and Jerry Lassoff, Richard Lavenstein, Tom and Diane Lekometros, Roni and Robert Lemle, Stephen Lesser, Robert Parke and John Libous, Yvonne Savaedra Limb, Renny Logan, Frank and Eve Lupo, Emanuela Frattini Magnusson, Karen Kuhlman and Greg Mahoney, Arthur Marcus, Edward Maxey, Calvin Tsao and Zack McKown; Rick, Nancy and Peter Michaelson; Larry and Lorraine Miller, Aprile Millo, Perry King and Santiago Miranda, Joe Molder, David Mullman, Bruce Nagel, Lewis Esson and Tim Pearce, Sandi and Keri Pei, Beth Rudin Pellegrini, James G. Pepper, Joel and Nancy Perlman, Liza Persky, Piero Portoghese, Rita and Mory Pynoos, Mark Randall, Robert Ransick, The Rechlers, Rodrigo and Adele Rodriques, Luis Miguel Rodriques-Villa, Louise Rosa, Dan Rowan, Jane Rozanski, Michael Rubin, Franklin Salasky, Rita Santambrogio, David Schutte, Christina Speligene and Phil Scheuer, June and David Schneider, Hope Cohn Schneider, Fredric Schwartz, Robert J. Shapiro, Hazel Siegel, Jeff Soref and John Silberman, Steve and Nina Solarz, Beth and Donald Straus, Jackie and Julian Taub, Andrew Tesoro, James Tigerman, Peter Elliot and Jorge Torregrossa, Ethan Robbins and Mary Travers, Henry van Ameringen, Steven Beer and Gaston van Duyse, Jan Willem van Lynden, Jean-George von Gerichten, Heather Watts, Doug and Sabra White, Bruce Wiener, Todd Williams, Paul Himmelstein and Beth Wladis, Barbara Mirecki and Ira Wool, Robert Wooley, and Jean-Bernard Wurm and Morris Zand.

Our most profound thanks to Susan Scott, Cathaline Cantalupo, and Alexandre Montagu, without whom our heads would not be above water.

Joseph Rosa

Foreword

Since the late 1960s the American architectural scene has been struggling to redefine the modern doctrine. This began with the publication of Robert Venturi's book *Complexity and Contradiction in Architecture* in 1966 and was followed in the early 1970s by a discourse mostly composed of self-referential historical debates between the "Grays" and the "Whites." However, in the late 1970s younger architects emerged, mostly schooled in or after 1968, looking to disciplines outside of architecture to inform their ideological framework for regenerating architecture. Over the years this has led to various architectural movements that have drawn from cinematography, phenomenology, semiotics, poststructuralism, and linguistics. More recently a new generation of architects has rejected the view that architecture must be textually informed through readings in literature; instead, they practice architecture that is tactilely informed through materials, massing, and color.

The work of Peter Stamberg and Paul Aferiat can be situated in this later group. Their architecture is more specifically informed by color and massing—more related to sculpture and painting than to an architectural precedent. During the seven years of their collaboration, their commissions have grown in scale from building interiors and furniture for Knoll to houses. Stamberg Aferiat's architecture is not about a return to the modernism of the recent past; it is an architecture that embraces the sensuous aesthetic of modernism. Their use of colors and tactile materials such as corrugated metal or plywood collaged with forms looks toward a modern aesthetic based on the visual sense: surface, saturation, texture, and light—descriptives more suited to defining art than architecture.

Because black-and-white photography was used to document the early buildings of the International Style in Europe, colored surfaces and tactile materials seemed alien to this idiom of smooth stucco and lath. Through magazines and exhibitions, photography was primarily responsible for informing the American public of this new architectural vocabulary, even though the European photographers at the time were novices in this new profession and its accompanying aesthetic. By the time the movement officially arrived in the United States in 1932, in the form of the landmark exhibition "Modern Architecture—International Exhibition," curated by Henry-Russell Hitchcock and Philip Johnson at the Museum of Modern Art in New York (and the later publication of *The International Style: Architecture since 1922*), the architecture had lost its political and social character, and all traces of color had faded too. Nowhere in the exhibition or the book was color ever addressed. This was an oversight of particular relevance since many architects who were featured, including Le Corbusier, Gerrit Rietveld, and Mies van der Rohe, had been using color in their architecture for many years.

In America architects and designers of modern houses have slowly been experimenting with color and its various applications. Color studies by Josef Albers and Johannes Itten have become essential tools in considering the use of contrasting colors of equal value on surfaces. But even with this new interest, color has usually been relegated to fabric for furnishings and rarely incorporated into architecture. And still today, with the exception of such figures as Luis Barragán and Ricardo Legorreta in Mexico, most architects' use of color as texture and surface has been minimal.

Stamberg Aferiat's interest in rethinking color as architecture has led them to search beyond the normative color theories of Albers and Itten. For them, the natural solution, besides the work of Barragán, was to be found in art. The work of Henri Matisse, in particular, has served as their inspiration, and that came about through David Hockney, who advised them to revisit Matisse's understanding of color. The colors used in the 1991 repainting of their loft/studio are co-opted from Matisse's 1947 painting *Luxe, Calme et Volupté*, and are a clear indication that their use of color is not random but very specific. Another example is seen in the Apartment for Tom and Linda Platt (1990), which is finished in a spectrum of greens. They select within the range of their choice of color or variety of colors, allowing these collectively to evoke a sense of light. This is most evident in the loft/ studio where the perimeter walls of a freestanding guest room are painted in a spectrum of yellow to orange so that the wall surfaces read as if one is continually washed in sunlight while the adjacent wall is in partial shade.

Although their bold use of color has become an identifying component of their architecture, not everything they do is color based. The Fifth Avenue apartment for a ceramic collector (1993) is finished in gradations of white, allowing the vast collection of Picasso pottery to take center stage. The pottery is displayed in niches that seem randomly carved out of a large volumetric wall that is slightly angled off the grid of the apartment. In contrast, an elegant copper awning hung from the ceiling spans the living/dining areas and acts as a light source. Stamberg Aferiat's use of a tactile material such as perforated copper allows the material's structural and aesthetic characteristics to be formally expressed. The same could be said of the manner in which corrugated metal is used as an exterior sheathing material at the Sycamore Creek House (1994) near Princeton, New Jersey. To articulate visually the extension from the house to Stamberg Aferiat's new addition, a transitional form was inserted, reminiscent of the original structure in massing and horizontally clad with corrugated aluminum to mirror the character of the house's wood clapboard siding. The architects' use of these materials as interior and exterior surfaces calls into consideration traditional

10

Foreword
Joseph
Rosa

perceptions of these materials and their functions. Evidently for Stamberg Aferiat this exploration into the connotational qualities of materials and colors is revealed through art.

Stamberg Aferiat's interest in the work of David Hockney and their subsequent friendship have played a significant role in their use of color and perception of movement through space. More specifically, it is Hockney's notion of reverse perspective (fracturing of space and volume) that has had a powerful influence on their work. Hockney's photographic collage *The Desk, July 1st, 1984* best illustrates his idea of reverse perspective, in which the front, sides, and top of the desk can be seen simultaneously. This multiple fracturing never allows the desk to lose its readability as a desk. This photographic collage is not about deconstructing an object as much as it is about a visual unfolding that presents a new and multidimensional world to the viewer.

Stamberg Aferiat's interpretation of Hockney's notion of reverse perspective can be seen intermittently in their works starting from 1990. The first to illustrate this was the Apartment for Tom and Linda Platt, where a perpendicular, cranked wall (which is slightly off the grid of the apartment) is anchored at opposite ends by a fireplace in the living room and a window in the dining room. The wall stops short of the ceiling plane and slopes down to its converging corner. The subsequent optical illusion perspectively extends the room as it diminishes its height, forcing a visual fracturing at the ceiling and wall plane.

This technique is also articulated on a larger scale in Stamberg Aferiat's residential work. The Sycamore Creek House addition and renovation illustrates how an existing building and site can generate a reverse perspective. The garage walls and roof ridge are purposefully misaligned, warping the roof plane. The garage walls refer back to the orthogonal grid of the original house, while the roof ridge mirrors the angle of the adjacent new living room wing. Another example of the site informing and fracturing additions to a preexisting structure can be seen in the Canterbury House (1994) in Watchung, New Jersey. The glass-enclosed living room addition to this Cartesian box (situated on a hill) comes to a point at the exterior balcony and resembles a bird in flight. The space of this addition is perspectively extended and warped, transforming the living room and balcony from a horizontal to a vertical section.

The sensuous, tactile qualities of Stamberg Aferiat's architecture look beyond the traditional modern doctrine, rejecting the notion of "form follows function." Moreover, it is through the interpretation of modern art that they have regenerated an architectural discourse that is informed by context, color, and client. In the future, when history unravels the struggles of the modern doctrine, it may reveal that color always belonged at the center of the dialogue.

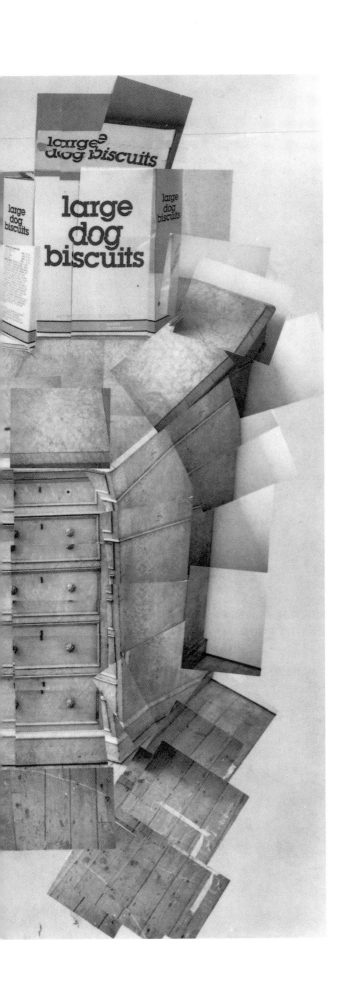

Foreword
Joseph
Rosa

David Hockney
"The Desk, July 1st 1984"
Photographic Collage, 48 1/2 x 46 1/2"
© David Hockney, 1984

Paul Goldberger

Introduction

Gentle modernism, thoughtful modernism, joyful modernism—
each of these phrases would be an oxymoron in most contexts,
and together they seem more contradictory still. Modernism is rarely
enough gentle, it is all too often not thoughtful, and even less fre-
quently, alas, is it visibly joyful. But these phrases describe the work of
Peter Stamberg and Paul Aferiat precisely. In the eight years of their
architectural partnership, they have produced a body of work that is
notable both for its relaxed ease and for its devotion to the modernist
ethos; more significant still, their architecture seems unburdened by any
sense of conflict between the demands of that ethos and the needs of
their clients. Stamberg and Aferiat approach their work with a generosity
of spirit that extends both to the architects who inspire them and to the
clients who pay them.

It is a telling fact of our time that the notion of architecture as
accommodating and the notion of architecture as intelligent
seem inconsistent, as if architects could only prove their mettle by demon-
strating indifference to the needs of their clients. Noble, heroic creators,
thrusting thunderbolts down from the Olympus of design toward cower-
ing clients grateful for the honor—somehow the mythology of the architect has not broken as far from this *Fountainhead*-induced model as we
might think. But Stamberg and Aferiat help us move away from it, under-
scoring its absurdity by their combination of rigorous intelligence and
conscientious commitment to the solution of specific problems, by their
exuberant love of the modernist legacy, and by their profound interest in
the lives and personalities of the people for whom they design.

Their approach stems in part from temperament—both architects
are gracious, precise in manner, and genuinely eager to listen—
and in part from a strategic awareness that genuine responsiveness was
the only way that two little-known, undercapitalized architects could
establish a practice. "We could not afford to walk away from jobs," Peter
Stamberg recalled not long ago. "Paul and I realized that we believed in
the power of architectural form, but that the only way we would ever
get to build any of it would be to fulfill clients' functional needs so daz-
zlingly well that they could see no other option."

Thus Stamberg and Aferiat convinced one client who came to
them seeking a colonial-style addition to an eighteenth-century
farmhouse to build something modern instead, and convinced another
client who initially disdained any serious, "high-design" efforts at all to
commission one of the firm's strongest and most assertive houses, the
Persky/Patton House on Shelter Island. The architects seem to approach
their clients as educators, if not, sometimes, almost as therapists,
patiently trying to understand their motivations and endeavoring to

explain their designs not as art objects primarily, but as solutions to problems that are very much the clients' own.

I focus so much on process here not to give short shrift to the product, but only to acknowledge the set of principles behind this architecture, and to underscore the importance of Stamberg and Aferiat in carving out what we might call a post-theoretical turf, defined not by dogma but by commitment to finding a way to solve problems without compromising the seriousness and integrity of the modernist aesthetic. To Stamberg and Aferiat the notion of accommodation does not mean an abandonment of aesthetic concerns, nor does it mean the opposite, a willingness to subjugate aesthetic judgments to clients' whims. Long ago Louis Kahn, when asked whether he preferred the client who knew precisely what he wanted or the client who left it all up to him, said he really liked neither type but sought instead the client "who knew what he aspired to." Stamberg and Aferiat have been unusually successful in finding clients who, like Kahn's, know what they aspire to, and these clients leave it to the architects to turn those aspirations into built form.

There is no easily defined Stamberg and Aferiat "look," yet there is a set of unifying ideas that give consistency to their architecture as a body of work. All of it emerges out of a certain exuberance—it is colorful, often intensely so, and active, though rarely to the point of appearing busy. Theirs is not minimalist modernism by any stretch of the imagination. They understand purity of space and form, but they do not believe it is communicated best by editing out every extraneous detail: On a continuum with Charles Moore at one end and John Pawson at the other, Stamberg and Aferiat, determined modernists though they are, might find themselves ending up closer to Moore. It is no accident that the loft in which the partners live and work is a virtual museum of modern chair design, not to mention chock full of art and painted in a brilliant palette. Stamberg and Aferiat wallow in the history of modern design with the joy, and at moments even the innocence, of eager graduate students, flush with excitement at being part of the world and determined to savor as much of it as they possibly can.

They are in many ways the sum of their major influences: the architects Charles Gwathmey and Richard Meier for whom Aferiat has worked, and the artist David Hockney, a longtime friend of both. Gwathmey and Meier are their Le Corbusier and Mies; Hockney is their Matisse. From Gwathmey came a respect for rigor and the importance of viewing space as an architectonic, almost tangible thing; from Meier came a love of composition and purity; and from Hockney came those qualities of exuberance that temper the others, and make them soar. Their loft, which is painted in neutral tones on all of its outside

16

Introduction
Paul
Goldberger

walls—the better to defer to the silver-gray light of New York and to the silvery tones of the skyline—possesses rich and intense colors in its interior walls, a kind of Hockney wrapped inside a Gwathmey: cool exterior, emotional interior, its architects eager to show that they are the bridge between the two.

Not all of Stamberg and Aferiat's work is quite so demonstrative of their own personalities, but all of it shows something of the partners' comfort with the heritage of recent modernist architecture. They are so comfortable with it, in fact, that they have made something of a subspecialty of renovating or adding to the work of Richard Meier, Aferiat's first employer. In three separate projects they have taken Meier work and redone it to meet the changing needs of the original client, making their mark while not obliterating Meier's own. Not an easy task when the architect and the architecture are as strongly defined and self-assured as Richard Meier. It would have been easier had these projects been for clients seeking to erase Meier's work (though hard to imagine Stamberg and Aferiat wanting to work under such circumstances), but in each of these instances, the clients valued Meier's design and sought an architect capable of respecting it.

Indeed, in the first Meier project Stamberg and Aferiat took on, an update of a 1977 apartment on Gramercy Park designed for Phil and Lucy Suarez, Paul Aferiat had been the original project architect under Meier. While he and Stamberg retained most of the architectural bones Meier had given the apartment, they added bright, almost Latin colors to the space through brilliantly colored furnishings and by way of a coat of yellow paint added to a beam Meier had thrust across the living room like a great gateway arch. The result is a space that seems, almost miraculously, to possess both Meier's serene coolness and an overlay of hot passions—to suggest emotions that are at once given free rein and held in check.

Meier No. 2 was a greater challenge: the Hoffman House in East Hampton, one of Meier's very earliest works, an essay in rotated geometries that, as Stamberg and Aferiat quickly realized, was like a closed system, a self-contained shape offering no logical route to expansion. Putting aside the initial instinct to add something altogether different from the original (something the client, who adored her nearly thirty-year-old house, would not accept in any event), the architects eventually figured out a way to, in effect, crack Meier's code by extending walls from the axes of two of Meier's rotated rectangles, yielding a new master bedroom wing and a larger living room. The work is remarkably discreet, paying homage to Meier by all but disappearing within his original scheme. This is not so much an addition as a rewriting of architectural history, making Meier's original concept bigger and considerably more gracious, but all blending in so seamlessly that it is difficult for the visitor now to distinguish between what was added in 1996 and what Meier himself did in 1967.

Stamberg and Aferiat's presence is somewhat easier to detect in the final Meier work, the additions to Clifty Creek Elementary School in the architecturally celebrated town of Columbus, Indiana—a project that not only marks their move into larger-scale work, but also puts them into that town's heady environment alongside work by not only their mentors Meier and Gwathmey, but also Eliel and Eero Saarinen, Robert Venturi, Cesar Pelli, Hardy Holzman Pfeiffer, I. M. Pei, and others. The charge here was to expand Meier's 1982 design and retrofit it to meet the standards of the Americans with Disabilities Act, which was accomplished by adding an elevator in a courtyard and stacks of classrooms at either end of a long axis, the whole neatly articulated to retain its scale and avoid any sense of overly long mass.

For all the fascination inherent in what seems to have become an ongoing relationship between Stamberg and Aferiat and Richard Meier's architecture, it is the non-Meier projects, of course, that show Stamberg and Aferiat's potential to a far greater degree. As a group, the firm's house designs are notable for a commitment to the notion that modernist form, so often (as in the Hoffman House) self-contained and acontextual, can in fact be deeply responsive to both context and program. Paradoxically, given how much their solution to the frustrating problem of expanding the Hoffman House was based on finding a way in which to respect the self-contained geometries of the plan, Stamberg and Aferiat's own plans are rarely self-contained, not at all closed, and generally not inward-looking at all.

They are, instead, shapes that derive from circumstance. In the case of the Sycamore Creek House (1994), near Princeton, for example, the fulfillment of a complicated program calling for the expansion of an eighteenth-century farmhouse and the provision of display space for a collection of twentieth-century art led to a solution of striking power and drama in which the interior of the farmhouse was expanded into a double-height library, while a new living room and master bedroom wing was built in a curving mass set beside the original wing, its axes arranged in careful geometric relationship to the original structure.

The design for the Bradbury/Jones House (1995) in East Hampton was based on what was, in effect, an opposite situation: a dramatic site in which the clients sought not a commanding presence but an understated one. Stamberg and Aferiat created a geometric form that appears minimal on approach but contains expansive, even soaring spaces within that take full advantage of the views. Here the modernist forms respond not only to the site, but in two different ways to the clients' fondness for aviation. A crow's nest reading retreat suggests an airport control tower, and from the side the overall form of the house, with its cantilevered deck, calls to mind, distantly but clearly, one of the great modernist houses, Purcell, Feick, and Elmslie's Bradley House of 1912, which appeared almost to fly off the coast at Woods Hole.

Curving forms join with boxy ones to create a sense of mass both in movement and at rest; surfaces of different materials and textures play off each other in carefully wrought composition; site and program are always uppermost. These things mark the new and striking design for the Persky/Patton House, which may turn out to be the partners' most complete and fully realized residential work. The designs for this house—actually a grouping including a main house, guest house, garage, and pool pavilion—seem to blend both geometric crispness with relaxed, gentle ease, and to be full of a love of materials and their relationship to the landscape. But these guiding principles, if they can be called that—the making of mass and composition that are both energetic and serene, the making of plan and space in response to site and program—can be said, truly, to sum up the design process that has always driven Stamberg and Aferiat, for whom modernism has seemed from the beginning to have represented both accommodation and aesthetic possibility. For these architects modernism is not aloof but engaged—connected to the land, to the city, to the past, and to the ongoing business of life.

Richard Meier

The art of architecture is taking many forms as we approach the millennium, but given the traditional constraints of program, site, schedule, and budget, the architect still hopes to achieve a work that will remain vital long after it is completed. The architect must realize that upon completion, his creation belongs to someone else, to the client, and that it is now out of his control and will go on to have a life of its own. When alterations become necessary due to program changes or other client needs, one hopes that the original conception will be treated with respect and integrity.

Peter Stamberg and Paul Aferiat have been selected to do renovations and/or additions to three of my buildings. In fact, to my knowledge, these are the only three projects of mine that have been altered in any way without my direct involvement, so it is a particularly unique situation that all three were done by the same architects. With my recommendation Stamberg and Aferiat received the commission for the renovation of the apartment I designed for Phil and Lucy Suarez in 1977 in New York. They did an outstanding job completing the kitchen and integrating their work in a respectful way with my original intervention. Because of this experience, in 1993 I recommended them to Anita Hoffman for the addition she was contemplating for her house in East Hampton, which I had designed in 1966. I also learned from Paul Aferiat that they had been selected as architects for the expansion of the Clifty Creek Elementary School in Columbus, Indiana, soon after they received this commission. In all three cases, I could not have hoped for these works to have been in better hands.

At both the Hoffman House and Clifty Creek Elementary School, sensitive, almost seamless additions have resulted. Stamberg and Aferiat brought their own vision to these projects rather than attempting mindless imitations. They were able to synthesize the overriding concepts of the buildings and expand and update them to satisfy changing needs.

In the Suarez Apartment renovation, they turned my definition of white as being all colors on its head by literally providing vibrant, pulsating colors instead. The bright yellow flying beam is an extension of the sunlight that I was attempting to bring into the apartment with glass block walls that allowed natural light to stream through.

The success of these three projects, as with all of Stamberg and Aferiat's work, lies in their dedication to the art of architecture, and, to paraphrase Louis Kahn, in their ability to listen to what a building wants to be.

New York, December 1996

Richard Meier

Hoffman House. East Hampton, New York, 1966-67

Photographs: Ezra Stoller © Esto

Richard Meier
Clifty Creek Elementary School. Columbus, Indiana, 1978-82
Photographs: Ezra Stoller © Esto

David Hockney

Color and perspective are not discussed much today by makers of images or by architects.

T.V. color seems to have made every place in the world look the same.

I tend to think people have color phobia. I was alone for awhile, defending the colorization of movies (they are only coloring a reproduction). Photography had drained color away. All the ancient world was colored—Egypt, Greece, pre-Columbian America. Somehow we have got it in our minds that color is "primitive."

Stamberg Aferiat stand against the beige monochrome of most interiors—color the exteriors as well, I would say, and I know they would agree.

Space + time, space + color. Can they really be separated?

As a new awareness of space emerges for us, color will be a bigger part of it. Keep working, Peter and Paul.

Los Angeles, November 1996

Charles Gwathmey

The architecture of Peter Stamberg and Paul Aferiat represents, in the most positive sense, the conflict between historical modernism and its extension. There is a clear grounding in the modernist plan/section aesthetic and the abstract and minimalist ethic of space/form articulation, overlaid with color saturation and layering, decorative intervention, material expression, and object manifestation, as well as a sense of humor and commentary.

The work embodies the dynamic speculation of collage and counterpoint, yet the question may be, is it too polite, discreet, and/or resolved? The intentions are clear, the sensibility is refined, the detailing is impeccable, the graphic is contrapuntal, the color is reinforcing, and there is an irrefutable sense of reconciliation. However, I suggest, *that* is the problem, not in a cosmic sense, but in a developmental sense. Would it be possible to reinforce the conflict inherent in collage and historical bridging by exploiting what one might call the implication of, or actual, irresolution?

Through education and practice, these architects know and believe in their historical roots as well as understand their obligation to speculate. Formally, there is the reference to a double-exposed or underexposed photograph. The question of choice is in the editing: How clear or how obscured is the overlay?

I have great admiration for the work and the architects. But, more importantly, I have greater faith in their future, because the rules are understood and there is the undeniable capability and desire to break them.

Stamberg and Aferiat are at a unique moment in their discovery process, where they can look with gratitude to the past and with uncontaminated optimism to the future. The dues have been paid, the commitment made; the obligation now is to read the cracks and shadows, be subversive, idealistic, and interrogative. Only in that way does one grow, and these architects are ready and able to do so.

New York, September 1996

Built

Hoffman House
Restoration and Additions
East Hampton, New York 1996

When the Hoffman House was finished in 1967, Richard Meier told his client that the design was complete and could never be added to. Over twenty-five years later, in 1994, Anita Hoffman called Meier and told him that the needs of her family had outgrown the house. She wanted to add to it. We were on the list of architects whom Meier suggested she call.

In studying the plan for this structure we came to feel that it was quite different from Meier's other houses. Unlike his other projects, which we think of as collages, we saw this design as a clear and complete, somewhat locked, geometric system. With a collage, no matter how perfectly balanced, there is usually an aspect that appears serendipitous, often leaving an opening for expansion. The plan for this house consisted of two exquisitely carved rectangles rotated about each other. The client felt that each room was too small, but was it possible to add to the house without destroying it? At first we could not see how. The plan seemed as tight as a drum. Looking at subsequent Meier designs we saw that, like this one, many of them sprouted landscape elements. When we extended the walls of the rectangles into the landscape, we saw that we had found the key and opened the system. The landscape elements looked as if they could have been there all along, and we could easily add to them without compromising the original design.

To the new element we added distinct volumes that contain a new master bedroom/bath and present a solid, unfenestrated facade to the street, continuing the direction of the original design. The old master bedroom was too small for its purpose, but with a little push to incorporate a new fireplace, it made a fine den/guest room. Given these two "new" bedrooms on the ground floor, we were free to transform the three small bedrooms upstairs into two larger rooms to achieve the four bedrooms requested. By completing the implied and overlapping rectangles of Meier's original design, we also were able to expand the living room, dining room, and kitchen.

*Hoffman
House*
1996
East Hampton
NY

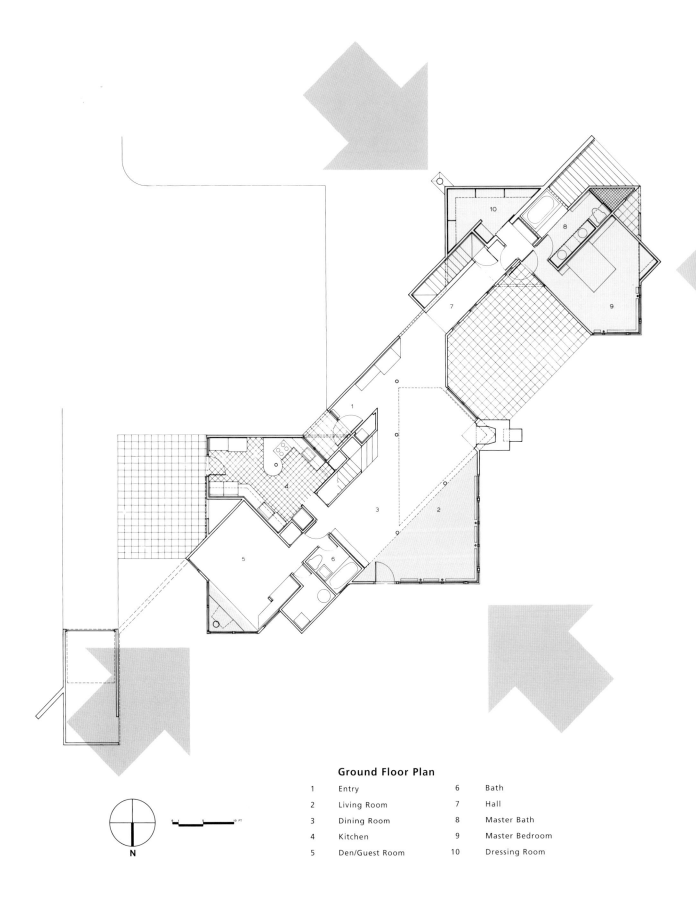

Ground Floor Plan

1	Entry	6	Bath
2	Living Room	7	Hall
3	Dining Room	8	Master Bath
4	Kitchen	9	Master Bedroom
5	Den/Guest Room	10	Dressing Room

N

0   5   10 FT

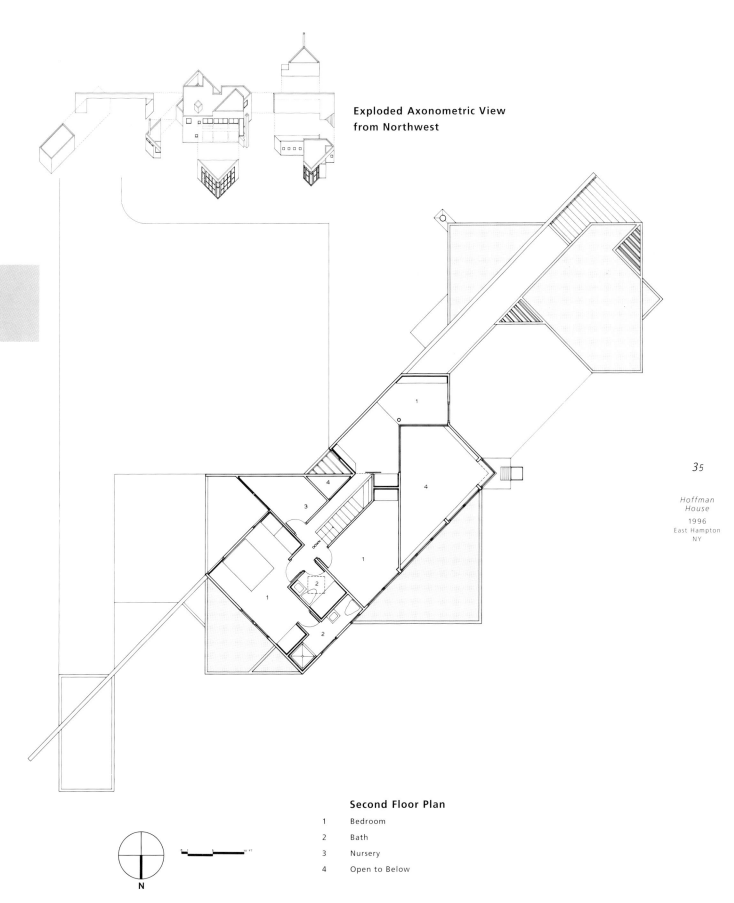

**Exploded Axonometric View
from Northwest**

*Hoffman
House*
1996
East Hampton
NY

N

Second Floor Plan

1   Bedroom

2   Bath

3   Nursery

4   Open to Below

*Hoffman
House*
1996
East Hampton
NY

Hoffman
House
1996
East Hampton
NY

Stamberg Aferiat Lounge Seating for Knoll 1994

Our process for designing sofas for Knoll began in June 1974 with Dino Gavina, the legendary design leader. Gavina saw modernism in a state of crisis. Conceived to fulfill the needs of a middle class created by the industrial revolution, modern design has been largely rejected by most of the population for whom it was created. Why, Gavina asked, were so many alienated by modern design? And of the few people who were not, why was it that too few of them could afford the relatively high price tag that comes with it? Finally, many who want and can afford modern design are not willing to wait for better products.

Bauhaus theory and design were based on societal changes caused by industrialism and on a vision of what the world would be like in seventy-five years. From today's vantage point we can see that some of these visions were accurate, but many were not. Suspecting that the inaccurate predictions had caused many problems, we decided to go back in our minds to the 1920s and look at the future using a knowledge of construction and production techniques that have become intrinsic today, but that at that time had not even been dreamed of. We would then base our designs on modernist theory as it related to those realities.

First, we examined joinery. With improved technologies many connections are stronger than the materials they connect. We realized that perpendicular, regular legs were a vestige of old needs, so we decided to angle and rotate the legs eccentrically. Second, seeing that upholstery had changed little since the invention of the sewing machine, and wanting to utilize new technologies, we aimed at minimizing handwork and looked for an industrially produced exoskeleton. Our short search turned up plywood, MDF, and honeycomb panels. We then looked at the work of Frank Lloyd Wright and Eileen Grey and designed a system of optional shelves for the sides and back of our sofa. The design changes radically with the addition of shelves. Finally, we developed six brilliant colors and three metallics for Knoll—colors inspired by Henri Matisse and David Hockney that we often use in our architecture.

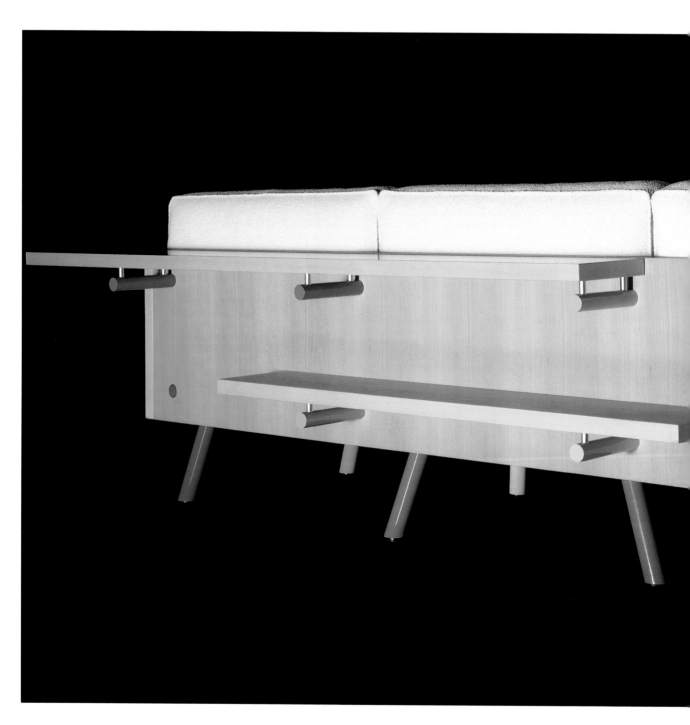

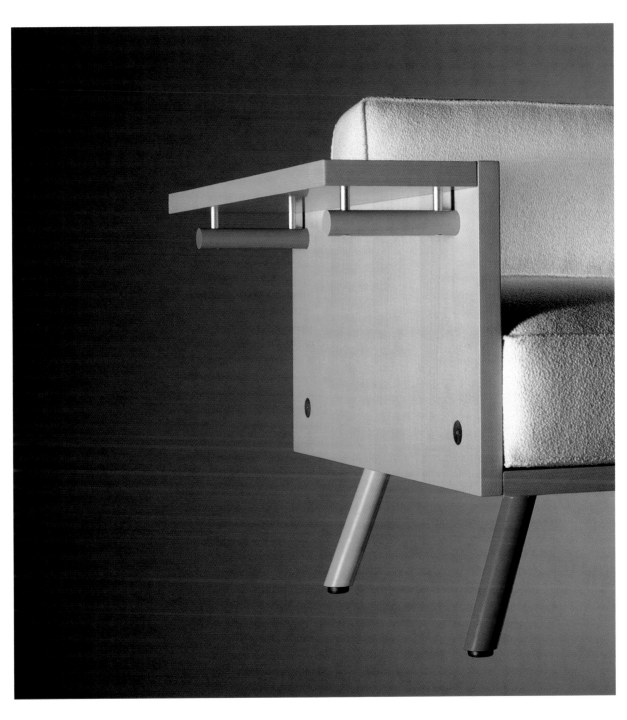

Lounge
Seating
for
Knoll
1994

Sycamore Creek House
Princeton, New Jersey 1994

Our clients requested an addition to and renovation of the 200-year-old farmhouse they had purchased two years before but had not yet moved into. The structure sits on thirty-two beautiful acres that include two ponds with wooded islands. Though badly maintained and modified over the years by previous owners, the old farmhouse had dignity in its age. The clients asked that the modifications respect the existing farmhouse and take advantage of the magnificent landscape. Because the members of the family were tall and they collected large-scale modern art, the low ceilings and introverted farmhouse needed some radical, yet careful, attention.

The first part of the program called for a large new living room and a new master bedroom suite scaled to our clients' (and their collection's) stature. The difficulty was at once to respect the farmhouse and to make it suitable for this family and its art collection. Rather than resort to imitating an old farmhouse, we recommended creating the spirit of a modern farmhouse. We did away with the ceiling in the old living room, thereby eliminating the former master bedroom on the second floor. This gave the house a double-height volume within the existing mass. The south half of the former living room became the double-height library; the balance of the space contains a reception room and circulation below and part of the master suite above. The new reception room spills into a new living room wing which, in turn, opens onto sweeping views of the landscape. The new master bedroom hovers above.

Rather than create an orthogonal, neoclassical forecourt, we placed the living room addition and the gable of the garage addition at 105.8 degrees to the main house and kept the floor plate of the garage on the orthogonal, thereby warping the planes of the garage roof. This dynamic new forecourt redefines the prominence of the original farmhouse.

The corrugated aluminum on the portion of the addition that connects the old house to the addition is our modern interpretation of the farmhouse's traditional clapboard.

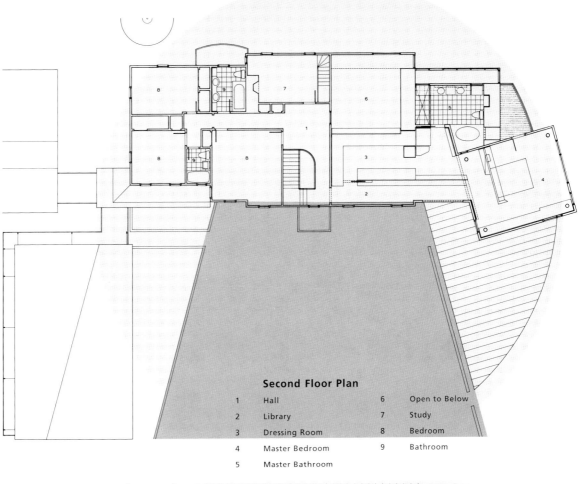

Second Floor Plan

1	Hall	6	Open to Below
2	Library	7	Study
3	Dressing Room	8	Bedroom
4	Master Bedroom	9	Bathroom
5	Master Bathroom		

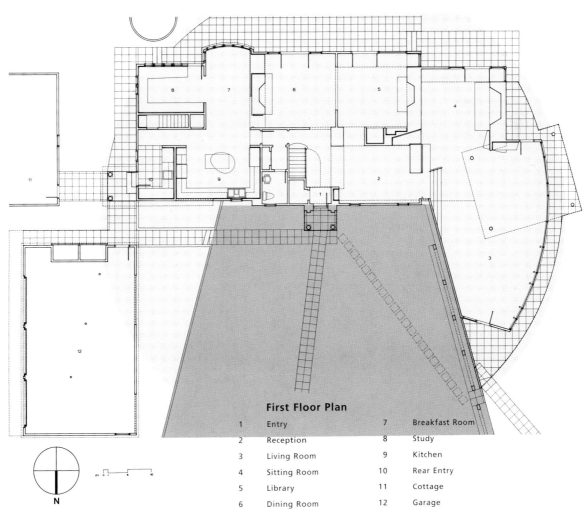

First Floor Plan

1	Entry	7	Breakfast Room
2	Reception	8	Study
3	Living Room	9	Kitchen
4	Sitting Room	10	Rear Entry
5	Library	11	Cottage
6	Dining Room	12	Garage

N

48

*Sycamore
Creek
House*

1994
Princeton
NJ

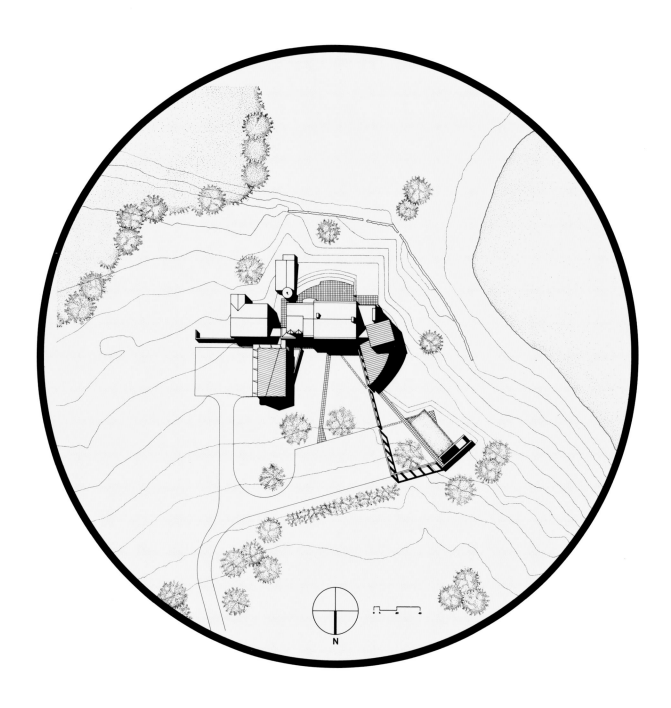

Site Plan

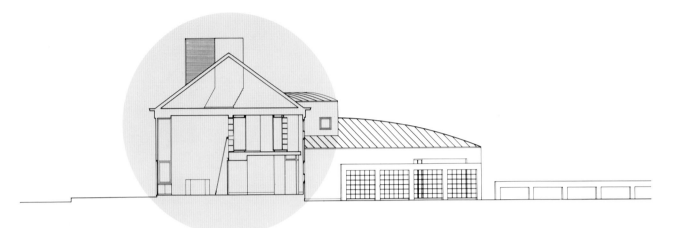

Cross Section Through Original House

51

Sycamore
Creek
House
1994
Princeton
NJ

Longitudinal Section Through New Living Room

Sycamore
Creek
House

1994
Princeton
NJ

Sycamore
Creek
House
1994
Princeton
NJ

Sycamore
Creek
House
1994
Princeton
NJ

59

Sycamore
Creek
House
1994
Princeton
NJ

Sycamore
Creek
House
1994
Princeton
NJ

Long Island Children's Museum — Pilot Project
Garden City, New York 1993

Conceived in 1990, the Long Island Children's Museum (LICM) opened its doors in November 1993 with a pilot space that is still in use. Intended as a temporary space for about two years while the museum formulated plans for a building of its own, the Long Island temporary Children's Museum (LItCM) has several tasks to achieve.

First, LItCM must teach its constituents (both children and parents) what a children's museum is: an institution for expanding children's horizons and teaching them lessons they might not learn in other environments. It aims to show parents that education occurs not only in schools or museums, but anywhere. Second, children's museums strive to show that museums are not boring or scary places, but places in which to engage the mind and have fun. Children's museums hope to spark children's imaginations and raise their design consciousness. Third, LItCM was built to represent LICM's first public presence, and consequently should act as a fund-raising tool toward construction of a permanent home.

The program called for four exhibits, an art program, an entry foyer with a ticket booth/sales area and a coat room, and administrative offices. Given the responsibility to spend contributors' money wisely and the expected two-year life span of the project, it was necessary to hold down costs as much as possible. Construction techniques and materials were kept very simple. The plan evolved from a single point, with walls either on a radius, or perpendicular or parallel to it, or in a rotation from it, or regular to the existing envelope. Corrugated steel and fiberglass were chosen to show how materials commonly assumed to be cheap and/or ugly could be rich and delightful. Also, fiberglass and Plexiglas reveal construction techniques, thus teaching children how framing, electricity, and plumbing are achieved. Strong color was used as an emotive force.

We conceived the entry wall as a Wall of Masterpieces. It consists of picture frames painted in a continuation of the museum's palette and containing homasote panels. The museum can display, on a rotating basis, work created by children in the art program. In addition, other images or objects can be inserted into the frames, turning things normally thought of as mundane into "masterpieces." For the opening of LItCM, the president of the board filled the wall with schematic sketches, construction documents, and progress photos of the board's "masterpiece" while it was under construction.

LItCM was constructed, painted, and carpeted for $15 per square foot. The existing ceiling and lighting were patched, filled in, and maintained.

Floor Plan

1   Entry

2   Reception

3   Coat Room

4   Administration

5   Exhibit Space

6   Storage

7   Art Room

N

64

*Long Island
Children's
Museum*
1993
Garden City
NY

66

*Long Island
Children's
Museum*
1993
Garden City
NY

A Ceramic Collector's Apartment New York 1993

We first heard the tale of "L'uovo di Colombo" from a Milanese friend. Asked to stand an egg on its end, an apparently impossible feat, Christopher Columbus placed a pinch of salt on the table. The egg stood easily in the bit of salt. "The moral," said our friend, "is that for many seemingly impossible tasks, there are actually simple solutions."

The varying entertaining needs that we had to accommodate in this fairly modest apartment seemed almost too diverse to fulfill. The apartment required space for intimate dinners with six to eight guests as well as for sit-down dinners for thirty and casual pre- and post-meal gathering. It also had to be able to accommodate up to 150 people for fund-raising functions. We had to keep several other factors in mind: the client's extensive collection of ceramics required a display system; a new master bath had to include a Japanese soaking tub; and both the kitchen and all closets needed to be enlarged.

To accommodate a thirty-foot table for thirty guests, the dining area would have to borrow space from the living room and the living room would have to borrow space elsewhere. To accommodate 150 people, even the living room and dining room combined would not suffice. The requirements were demanding, but the solution was simple: archways between the living room, foyer, and dining room were removed to create a single large space. To organize the disparate wall planes revealed in removing the archways, we built a new sculptural element that stands away from the existing wall. It incorporates display niches for the ceramics collection, with uplighting as well as general illumination. Half of the wall separating the living room from the master bedroom became a large pivoting panel. When the panel sits on the east-west axis, the room configuration remains as it had been. When the panel pivots to the north-south axis, more than 250 square feet are added to the living room by borrowing space from the master bedroom. If the banquet table is in place, or when the apartment needs to accommodate 150, the panel pivots south, and the living room expands into the borrowed space. Overhead, a thirty-foot-long custom copper-mesh light canopy defines the space for the banquet table below. It also makes the enlarged space more intimate when the room returns to its typical function.

A small kitchen and a maid's room were combined to create a large kitchen. The master bath was enlarged for the soaking tub. Closets were expanded. In an important visual and symbolic gesture, an oddly shaped column at the intersection of the living room, master bedroom, and solarium was reshaped into an egg, as was the kitchen island. Both were created in honor of "L'uovo di Colombo."

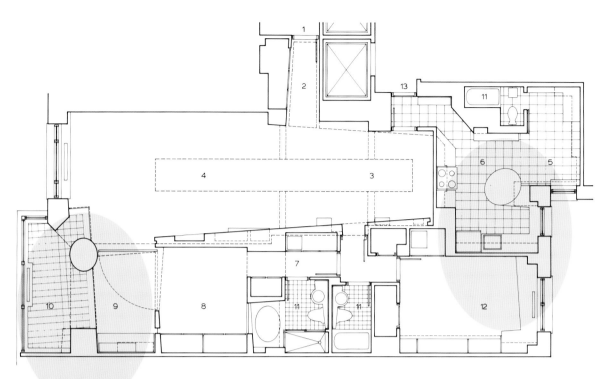

Renovation Plan

1	Entry	8	Master Bedroom
2	Entry Hall	9	Alcove
3	Dining Room	10	Solarium
4	Living Room	11	Bathroom
5	Study	12	Guest Bedroom
6	Kitchen	13	Service
7	Bedroom Hall	14	Maid's Room

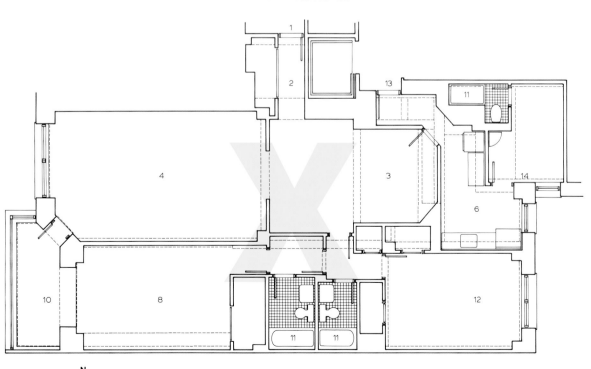

N

Original Plan

A
Ceramic
Collector's
Apartment
1993
New York

A
Ceramic
Collector's
Apartment
1993
New York

McCabe & Company
New York 1991

A tight schedule, a limited budget, and the need to project the image of a maverick advertising agency whose work is substantial, classic, and cutting edge were the driving forces behind the design of these temporary offices in sublet space for the new McCabe & Company. Given the constraints, we opted to aim for simplicity and order—but with dramatic twists and highlights.

Spending less than $18 per square foot on construction and furnishings, we were able to create and implement the design while the office functioned around a crew of carpenters, electricians, painters, and cabinetmakers.

McCabe & Company, founded by legendary adman Ed McCabe (formerly of Scali McCabe Sloves), opened on a Monday morning. McCabe called us that afternoon to ask us to design and build around the working agency. The walls, six of the private offices, and the workroom were retained. Drywall partition was added to create workstations, a conference room, and additional office space. Inexpensive, oriented strand board was used for the reception desk and custom cabinetry, while Apple-ply was used for the custom conference table. Strong yellow paint was used at the entry, an allusion to the heat of the sun and to an apocalyptic vision. Le Corbusier chairs in the reception area are a reminder of McCabe's famous ads for Maxell. The purple leather was chosen as a twist on a classic. During the short construction period the office staff grew from six to twenty-six. As the sublet drew to a close, McCabe & Company had not found a space they liked better. So, these temporary offices have become permanent—at least until the firm outgrows them.

Floor Plan

1	Elevator Lobby	8	Open Work Stations
2	Entry	9	Gallery
3	Reception	10	Kitchen/Workroom
4	Chairman's Office	11	Conference
5	President's Office	12	Storage
6	Secretary's Office	13	Terrace
7	Office		

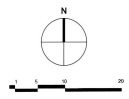

N

1 5 10   20

*McCabe
&
Company*
1991
New York

Stamberg Aferiat

Loft

New York 1976– (Painted 1991)

In 1976 both of us were just a few years out of school and struggling to get by on the income of young architects. Paul was working for Richard Meier and Peter was building do-it-yourself furniture for books and magazine articles. We were looking for the cheapest place we could find to live in Manhattan. The place also had to be big enough for a wood shop. An advertisement in the *Village Voice* brought us to a half-empty loft building in a deserted neighborhood. The space had no running water and only DC current. With a tiny budget, we brought in water and power and put up metal studs and some drywall. Over time the drywall was finished and, bit by bit, taped and spackled. Eventually a floor was laid, in two parts over several years.

> Our starting point was the realization that the views were most spectacular from close to the windows, so we would conceal the views until visitors were farther into the space than the entry. We designed the walls to create objects within the space and lots of storage and to define a bedroom, a bathroom, a kitchen, and a place for friends to stay. Walls were kept away from the windows to preserve the panoramic views; and, where possible, they were not built to the ceiling in order to maintain the loftlike, spacious feeling. Flying beams carried power and phone lines between the objects. Finally, in 1991, fourteen years after we moved in, we painted all the walls in colors inspired by David Hockney and Henri Matisse, a signature for which we are now known.

We had begun to collect twentieth-century furniture and art even before we met, but the collection increased geometrically when we became a team.

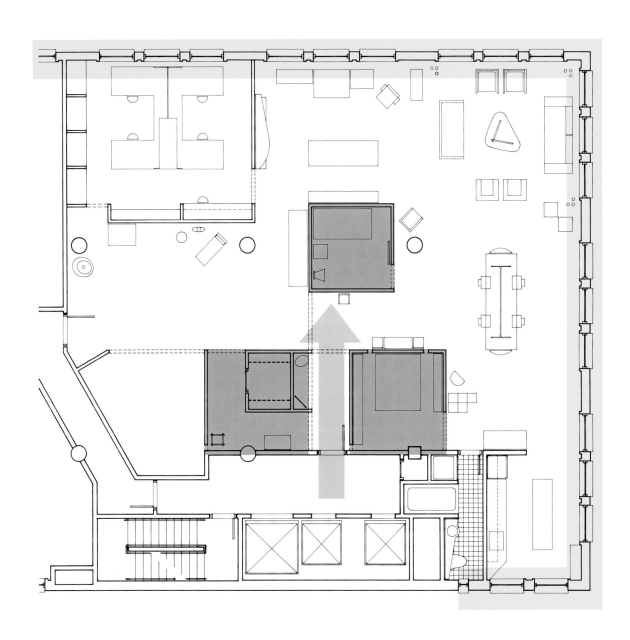

N

0 1   5   10

82

Stamberg
Aferiat
Loft
1976-1991
New York

*Stamberg
Aferiat
Loft*
1976-1991
New York

86

Stamberg
Aferiat
Loft
1976-1991
New York

Nelson/Sarna
Apartment Renovation
New York 1991

An exciting view of the East River inspired the clients to renovate this apartment on New York's Upper East Side. Several years before, they had already joined two apartments in this postwar building to create a three-bedroom home. When an adjoining two-room apartment became available it provided an opportunity to add a guest room/study, family room with wet bar and concealed TV/stereo equipment, bathroom, laundry room, and as much storage as possible. In addition, our clients requested that we work toward overcoming the lined-up, shoe box effect inherent in too many postwar buildings.

> Viewed from the windows of the apartment the East River seems to be running directly toward it. We usually think of the East River as running along a straight north-south axis, but barely in sight of the apartment is an often ignored bend in the river that creates this curious sensation. Although this view is very exciting, it is also very disorienting. The curved walls, soffits, and cabinetry in the apartment reinforce this all-but-invisible river bend, discreetly transforming what had been an unsettling view into one that is simultaneously breathtaking and peaceful.

The gallery's dropped and angled soffit ties the existing space to the addition. It also modulates the ceiling height while foreshortening the previously long, narrow rooms to more appropriate proportions. The curves and angles become sculptural elements that are strong enough to mitigate the banality of the original structure. By disengaging and rounding a previously square column, we further transformed the space from that of a typical apartment to one resembling a loft.

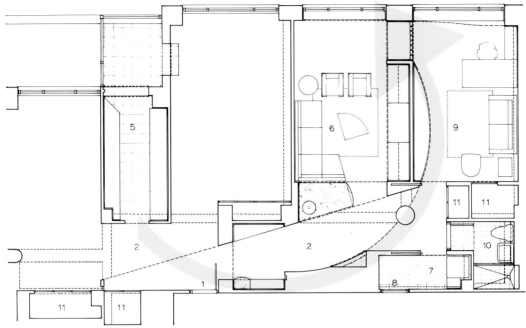

Renovation Plan

1	Entry	7	Laundry
2	Foyer/Gallery	8	Service
3	Living Room	9	Study/Bedroom
4	Dining Room	10	Bath
5	Kitchen	11	Closet
6	Family Room		

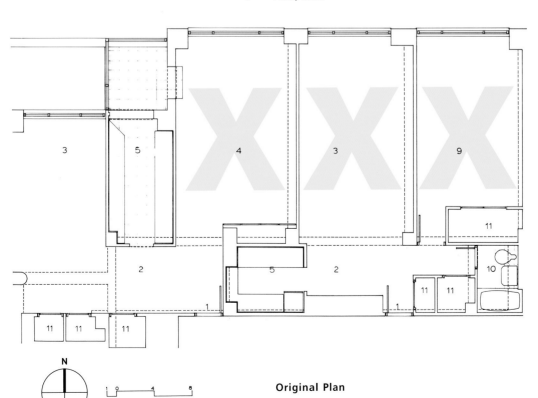

Original Plan

N

Nelson/Sarna
Apartment
1991
New York

92

Nelson/Sarna
Apartment
1991
New York

Apartment for Tom and Linda Platt
New York 1990

Located on the top floor of a splendid old residential building on Park Avenue, this apartment was purchased by a husband and wife fashion design team because of its relative proximity to their Seventh Avenue workshops and showroom. Aside from its location, there were few things they liked about the apartment. Their requests to us were to make the entry dramatic; make the apartment feel larger; design an unusual fireplace; add a powder room; create a modern, efficient kitchen; and increase clothing storage space.

The apartment was entirely gutted. Where there had been a small closet, a curved powder room was added. The dining room was opened up to the foyer so that both would feel bigger. To create a new and better kitchen, space was borrowed from the bedroom closets; to improve the bedroom closets, space was borrowed from the old kitchen. Most significant, a cranked, detached, and sculpted wall was added to clarify circulation from the entry foyer to the living room and back to the dining room, keeping the bedroom a private area. Both the cranked wall and the new powder room were detailed to read as objects inserted into the space.

To make the apartment feel larger than its fairly small 850 square feet, the top of the cranked wall was sloped into a forced perspective. The top of the wall carries concealed incandescent cove lighting that discreetly illuminates the path from the entry, past the dining room and into the living room. The wall is animated with recessed display niches and terminates at the midpoint of the living room with a fireplace mantel crafted of a gunblue, hand-ground steel plate attached to the wall with galvanized steel and brass fasteners.

The cabinetry of the simple galleylike kitchen and the living room is constructed of Finnish plywood. All wall surfaces are painted—new construction in strong shades of green in contrast to the very pale green of the original apartment shell. The bathrooms use industrial materials and simple black-and-white tiles to belie their modest scale.

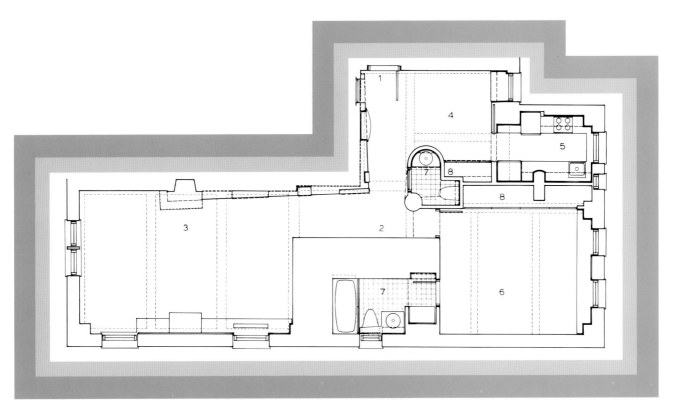

Renovation Plan

1	Entry	5	Kitchen
2	Foyer	6	Bedroom
3	Living Room	7	Bath
4	Dining Room	8	Closet

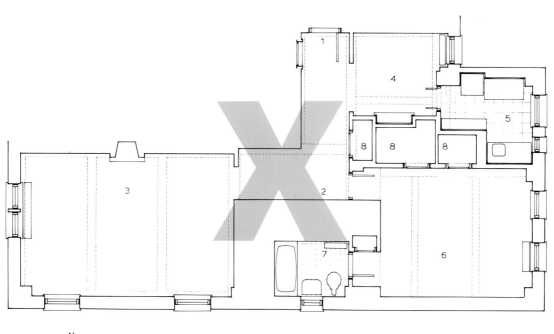

N

Original Plan

*Apartment
for
Tom and
Linda Platt*
1990
New York

Apartment
for
Tom and
Linda Platt
1990
New York

*Apartment
for
Tom and
Linda Platt*
1990
New York

Suarez Apartment
New York 1990

Twelve years after commissioning Richard Meier to design their apartment in 1977, our clients Phil and Lucy Suarez decided some changes and enhancements were due. Paul, who had been the original project architect at Meier's office, knew which important features of the original design had to be treated with care as well as those areas where the apartment would be able to grow. The clients requested that we respect this Meier gem while making the apartment more of a home for them, and they gave us the freedom to explore our own architectural vision.

We first tackled the parts of the apartment that had not been part of the original renovation, turning three small rooms into one large kitchen and creating a gym and steam room from an unused small bedroom and a bathroom. The original bathrooms were totally remodeled. New cabinet work was added. The biggest change to the pristine white Meier environment was the overlay of a bold color palette that reflects the animated personalities of our clients. As with many of our projects, we took our colors from Matisse to articulate Meier's original architectural interventions.

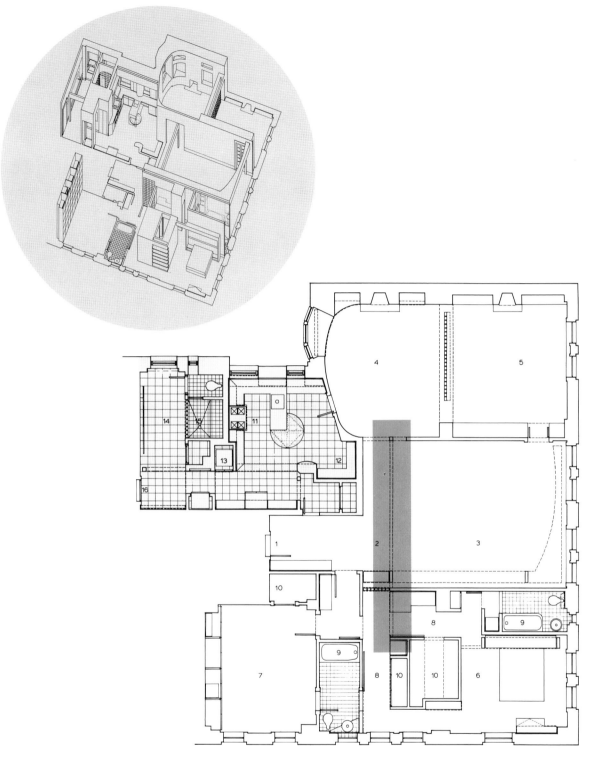

Floor Plan

1	Entry	9	Bath
2	Foyer	10	Closet
3	Living Room	11	Kitchen
4	Dining Room	12	Pantry
5	Library	13	Laundry
6	Master Bedroom	14	Exercise
7	Guest	15	Steam Room
8	Dressing	16	Service

N

Suarez
Apartment
1990
New York

Suarez
Apartment
1990
New York

*Suarez
Apartment*
1990
New York

Suarez
Apartment
1990
New York

Shumsky/Kronick
Apartment New York
1989

A busy professional couple who share the hobby of cooking purchased this apartment in a 1920s residential building on Manhattan's Upper East Side. It had large but dark reception spaces and an equally dark but small kitchen. By annexing a quadrant of the dining room and relocating the service entry, a large working kitchen was created. The new kitchen centers around a built-in granite table and hutch that displays the clients' collection of decorative housewares. Light brightens the reception rooms as a result of increasing the width of entryways and slicing a narrow horizontal slot in the top of the wall separating the newly reapportioned dining room and the living room. The slot not only allows southern light to penetrate deep into the apartment, but creates an extended sightline from one room to the next, increasing the spatial dimension of both rooms. The newly renovated master bathroom satisfies the request to accommodate a double vanity and shower while referring to typical 1920s black-and-white bathrooms in an updated fashion.

The colors for the apartment were taken from Matisse's *Two Girls, Red and Blue Background* (1947). They identify the new architectural elements, which contrast with the neutral color used on the apartment's existing classical elements.

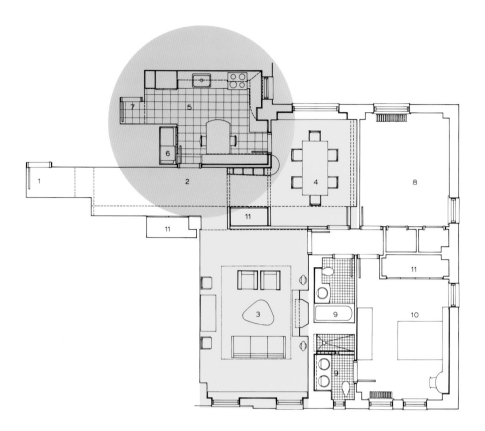

Renovation Plan

1	Entry	7	Service
2	Foyer	8	Study
3	Living Room	9	Bath
4	Dining Room	10	Master Bedroom
5	Kitchen	11	Closet
6	Laundry		

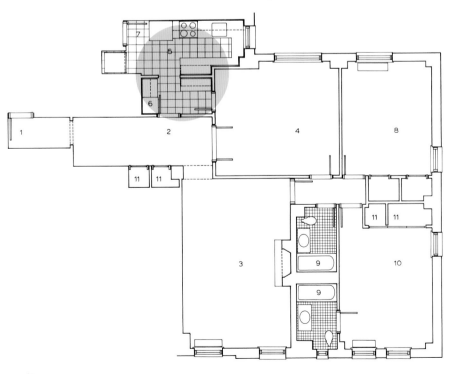

Original Plan

*Shumsky/
Kronick
Apartment*
1989
New York

Shumsky/
Kronick
Apartment
1989
New York

Kraus Apartment
New York 1988

This was "point zero," the very first residential project we designed as a team. Jill and Peter Kraus were two of our closest friends. About to outgrow an apartment ten blocks away, the Krauses purchased this prewar apartment despite its two shortcomings but with the faith that we could find a solution. The kitchen and two maid's rooms were Dickensian, and there was no playroom for their two sons. By borrowing two feet from the dining room, moving the kitchen next to it, and rotating the remaining two rooms ninety degrees to create a maid's room/bath (with two windows) and a playroom, the shortcomings were eliminated.

Working with a tight budget that was mostly devoted to needed reconfiguration, we then concentrated the remaining budget on the entry. Supported by adventuresome and visually sophisticated clients, the use of strong color in the Kraus Apartment is proof of the saying that paint is the least expensive architecture.

*Kraus
Apartment*
1988
New York

Wright Line Showroom Chicago, Illinois 1985

Down the two-block-long corridors of the Chicago Merchandise Mart, behind the glass walls of hundreds of showrooms, are more office furniture and supplies than most people care to see in a lifetime. With so many showrooms competing for buyers' limited time, how does a company attract visitors to its showroom, especially when the company is not well known and aesthetic aspects of design are not among its high priorities?

The answer is to defy conventional wisdom. Rather than using transparent front walls, make them opaque. Rather than painting the walls neutral white, gray, or beige, hand paint them with an aggressive pattern (we chose a notebook pattern as a parallel to the company's main product line—software filing devices, or computer "notebooks"). Rather than displaying products in the form in which they are actually sold, paint them in colors no one will actually buy, or make them stars of animated films shown on television monitors. Rather than painting the rough industrial ceiling black to hide its flaws, paint it white to feature them. But, most important, rather than designing for ease of production, as one does with the products, create a plan with strong and unbroken geometry and symmetry.

That is, create order and make the design rigorous.

Following this formula, Wright Line broke all records during the intensely competitive market week. People flooded to the showroom, and once inside, learned about the products.

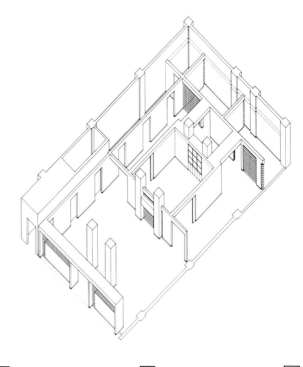

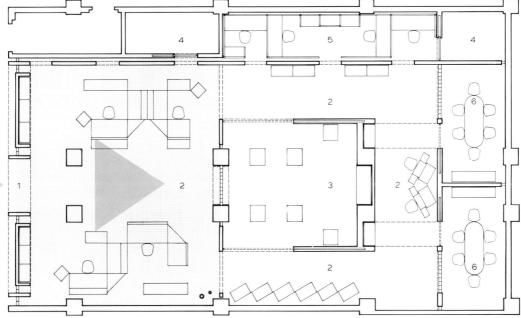

Floor Plan

1   Entry

2   Display

3   Conference

4   Storage

5   Enhancement Display

6   Meeting Room

N

0 1   5   10 FT

124

*Wright Line
Showroom*
1985
Chicago
IL

*Wright Line
Showroom*
1985
Chicago
IL

Projects

Persky/Patton House
Shelter Island, New York 1996

Our clients' search for land had one main focus: a dock for their newly restored, 50-year-old Norwegian sailboat, *Lulu*. When they showed us the hillside site, two features struck us immediately. First, its buildable width is only 35 feet. Second, the property has a stand of 60- to 70-foot-tall pine trees that are more reminiscent of the Adirondacks than of the sandy beaches, potato fields, and scrub oak of eastern Long Island.

The site's narrowness led to the development of a linear scheme of three detached structures connected by a strong organizational axis. Arranged in descending order on the hillside, the structures resemble an Adirondack camp. *Lulu*, bobbing at her dock, inspired the roof forms of all three structures, which are designed to recall wind-filled sails. The stays of *Lulu's* mast inspired cable supports for the entry awning on the north and the sun screens on the south. In plan, the "prow" of the main house faces land, while the "stern" faces the sea, like a boat docked in a harbor.

Since the property slopes down to the bay, we developed a split-level parti that placed the entry on grade with the north face of the house, thereby establishing an intermediate level. From this level one can ascend a half-flight of stairs to the master bedroom suite or descend a half-flight to the living room, dining room, and kitchen. Both husband and wife are remarkable chefs and enjoy spending time in the kitchen, so the living room, dining room, and kitchen work as one space but maintain separate identities. The clients requested that guests be accommodated in a separate guest pavilion with a simpler structure and finishes than those of the main house, a strategy that was both gracious and economical.

To build this new house, our clients left behind a weekend house across the bay that we had renovated five years before. They asked that several aspects of the first house accompany them to the new site; therefore, the double-height living room adjoins the kitchen and dining room on the ground floor, as in the previous house. The timber-frame construction is also repeated.

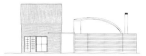

North Elevation

West Elevation

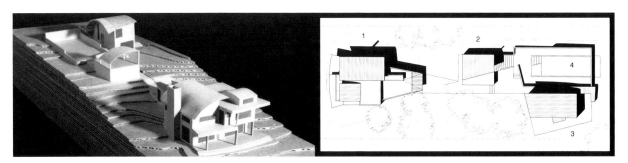

ABOVE RIGHT:

Site Plan

1   Main House
2   Garage/Pool Pavilion
3   Guest House/Studio
4   Pool

East Elevation

South Elevation

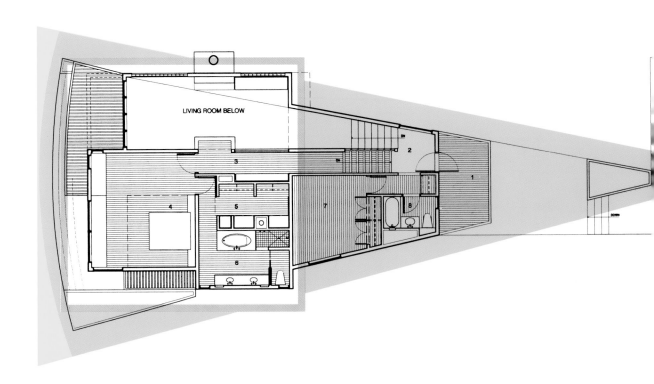

LIVING ROOM BELOW

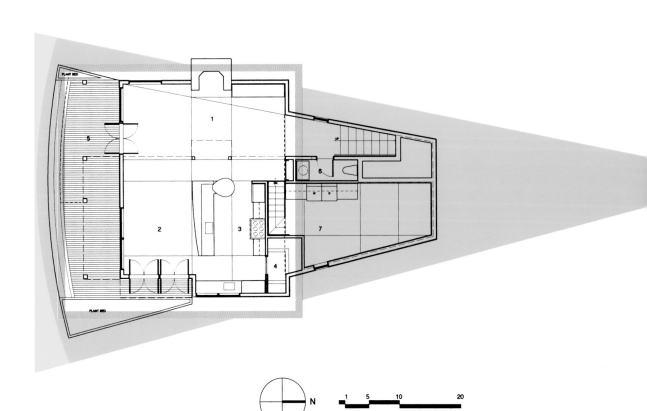

PLANT BED

PLANT BED

N

1 5 10 20

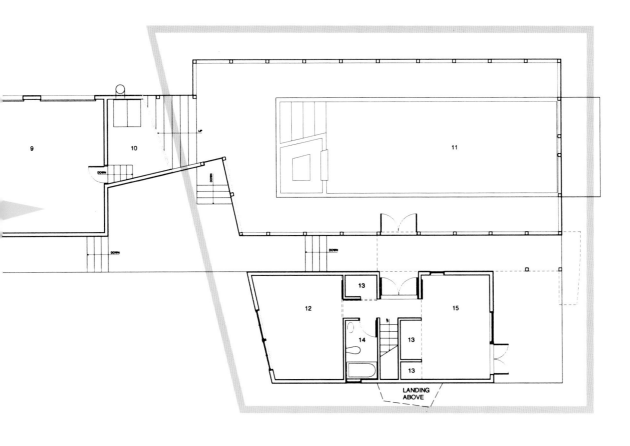

Persky/Patton
House
1996
Shelter Island
NY

Second Floor Plan

1	Covered Porch	9	Garage
2	Entry	10	Mechanical Room
3	Hall	11	Pool
4	Master Bedroom	12	Bedroom
5	Dressing Room	13	Closet
6	Master Bath	14	Bath
7	Guest Bedroom	15	Studio
8	Guest Bath		

Ground Floor Plan

1	Living Room
2	Dining Area
3	Kitchen
4	Pantry
5	Porch
6	Lavatory
7	Basement/Storage

Chiat House
Sagaponack, New York 1995-

When we were first approached to design a new beach house for these clients, we were told that no other architects would be interviewed. But it took us little time to figure out that we had stiffer competition than another firm: the beach house that our clients had been renting was actually a collection of exquisite old barn structures that had been gathered from around the Northeast, reassembled, and sited with perfectly flawless minimalism. When they told us that they would be happy with just the living room barn if it had a sleeping balcony and library balcony added—as well as a kitchen and more light—we were quite sure they understated the case. First, we felt that recreating a barn would be too nostalgic for a couple who had a remarkable contemporary art collection. Second, we realized that if balconies big enough for sleeping and for a library were inserted into a barn similar to the one they rented, the dramatic volume would be so consumed that all barn feeling would be gone.

The house consists of three distinct volumes. The primary volume is a modern interpretation of a hay barn. As many hay barns are raised off the ground one floor level to allow air circulation, here glass encloses a light-filled garden level. The upper level consists of two relatively small balconies connected by a glass bridge. The small bedroom balcony feeds to a larger space outside the volume of the barn to create a better-sized bedroom; the kitchen sits below. These are both contained in an adjacent silo-like volume. The library balcony opens onto a roof deck above the third volume, a boat-shaped guest room wing. Fenestration focuses north and south, toward the ocean and wetlands and away from the neighbors. Landscape walls, a pergola, and privet shrub walls form a circumference around the house to create privacy. A separate garage connects to the main house by a covered walkway.

North Elevation

West Elevation

East Elevation

South Elevation

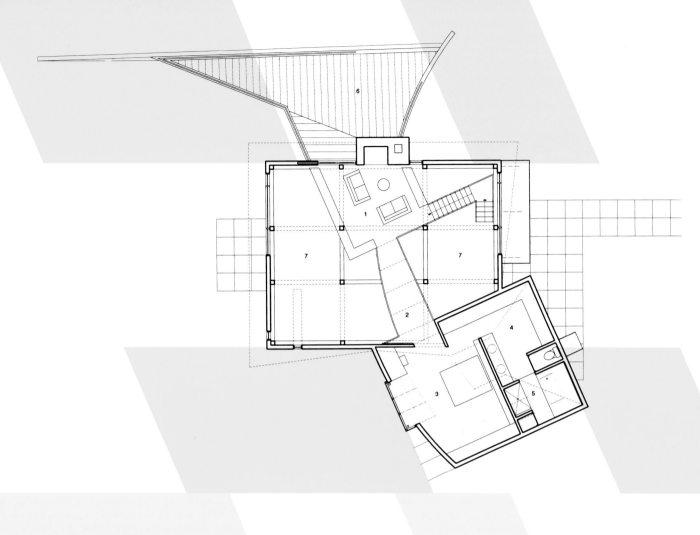

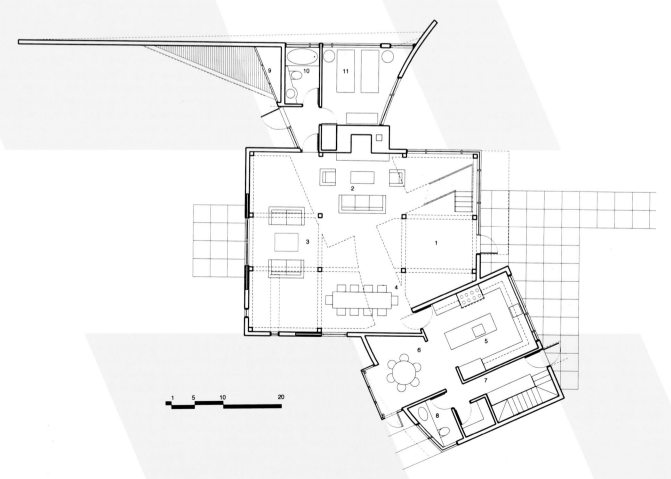

1   5   10   20

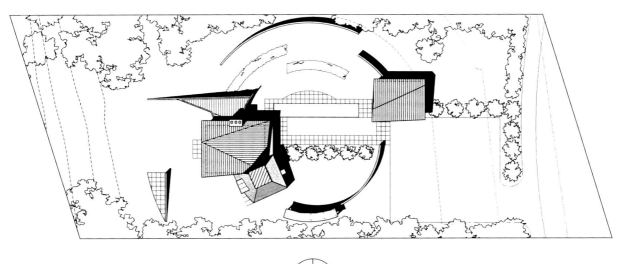

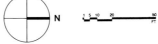

Site Plan

Chiat House
1995
Sagaponack
NY

OPPOSITE PAGE:

Second Floor Plan

1   Library

2   Bridge

3   Master Bedroom

4   Dressing Room

5   Master Bath

6   Deck

7   Open to Below

Ground Floor Plan

1	Entry	7	Entry Hall
2	Sitting Area	8	Powder Room
3	Living Area	9	Storage
4	Dining Area	10	Guest Bathroom
5	Kitchen	11	Guest Bedroom
6	Breakfast Room		

Bradbury/Jones House East Hampton, New York 1995-

With weekends filled with visits from friends and family members, our clients asked for a five-bedroom house with a great kitchen. Since they are avid tennis players and swimmers, their program called for a pool and tennis court on the site as well as a gym within the house. They spoke of their love of soaring spaces and aviation and made a very distinctive request to accommodate their small but growing collection of vintage and new cars.

The view from the wooded and dramatically sloped site toward the Atlantic Ocean, a few miles away, is wonderful. Approached from the lower elevation, the site made a fairly imposing design almost inevitable. This presented just one problem: such an imposing house would be totally inappropriate for the clients. Our challenge was to design a large house on a prominent site that would take maximum advantage of the vistas yet still maintain a discreet scale on the approach side.

To accomplish this, our scheme has the driveway rise against the south and then east borders of the site. Existing foliage shields the house from view until visitors are quite close. The first sight of the structure is the minimal, single-story entrance elevation on the northeast. Then, once one steps inside, the spaces and view explode: the guest wing fans out to the south and the soaring living spaces occupy the center. The master bedroom suite to the north is buffered by a crow's nest reading retreat. Its form suggests an airport control tower, addressing our clients' affinity for aviation.

One additional, and seemingly impossible, request was to make the six-car garage as unobtrusive as possible. By configuring it under the guest wing and stacking three bays in front of another three bays, we made the garage all but invisible—the three doors cannot be seen until the turn-off in the driveway.

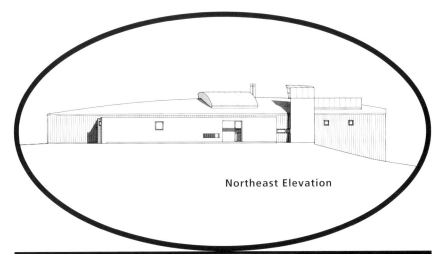

Northeast Elevation

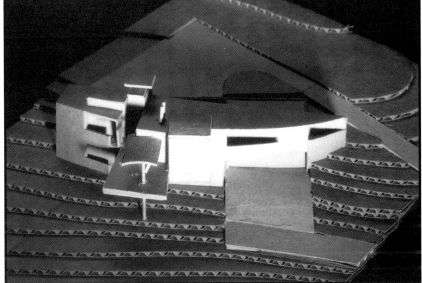

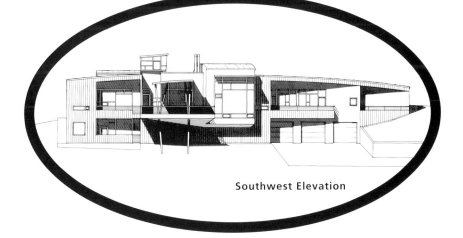

Southwest Elevation

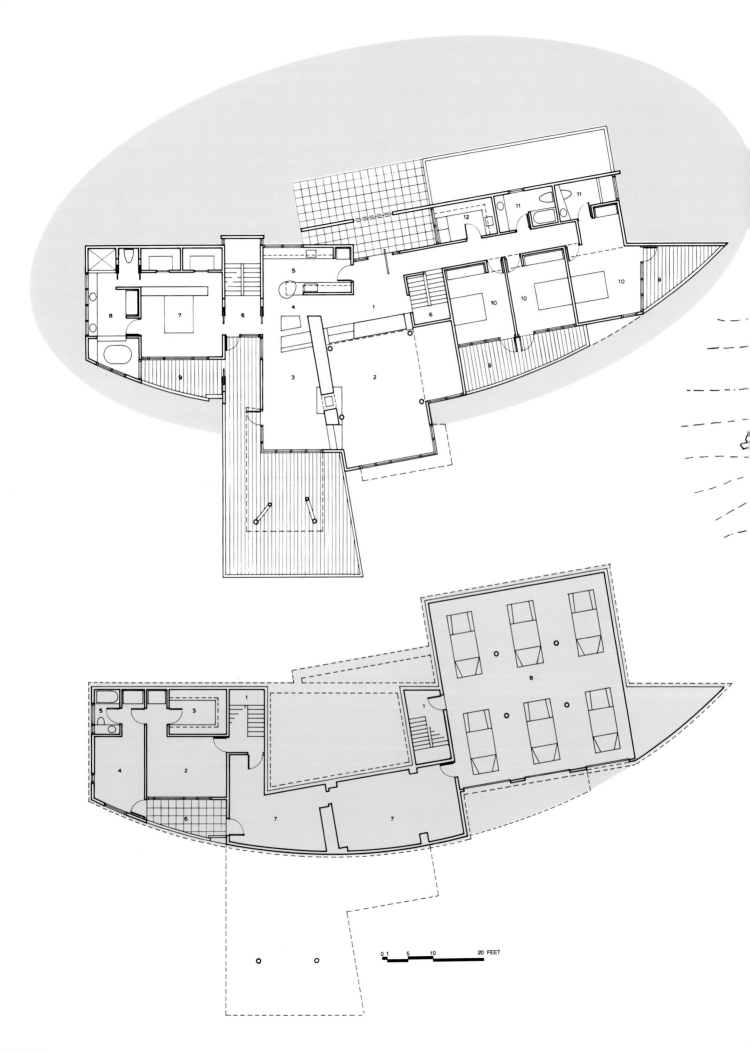

0 1 5   10   20 FEET

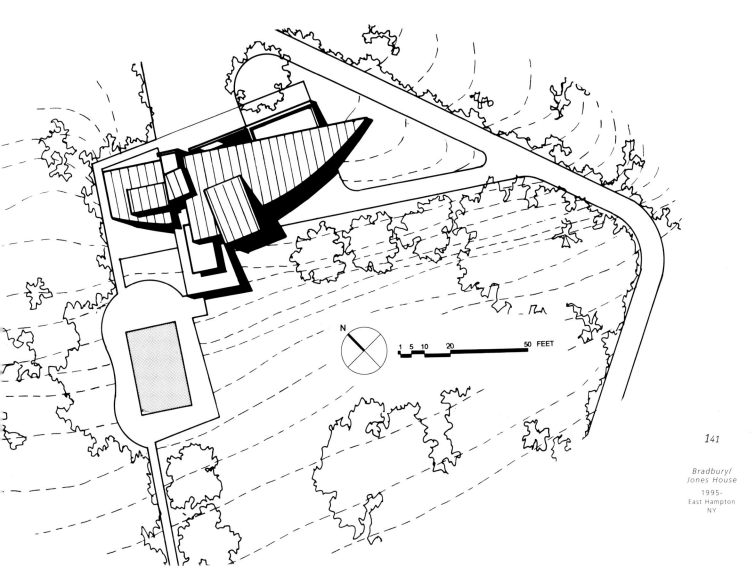

Site Plan

OPPOSITE PAGE:

Second Floor Plan

1	Entry	7	Master Bedroom
2	Living Room	8	Master Bathroom
3	Dining Room	9	Deck
4	Breakfast Area	10	Bedroom
5	Kitchen	11	Bathroom
6	Stair Hall	12	Laundry

Ground Floor Plan

1   Stair Hall
2   Study
3   Storage
4   Gym
5   Bathroom
6   Terrace
7   Mechanical Room
8   Garage

Canterbury House
Watchung, New Jersey 1994

In preliminary design meetings for this three-acre site in suburban New Jersey with a view of New York Harbor and the Verrazano Bridge twenty miles away, our clients asked us to let our imaginations soar. They requested a house for themselves and visiting children and grandchildren, as well as space for an art collection that includes works on paper by Matisse and American Futurist paintings, collages, and sculpture. They also asked for a secluded, but central, study for the husband and a completely separate painting studio for the wife.

The design pinwheels around a conical entry tower anchored on one side by the guest bedroom wing and balanced on the other by the soaring living room/dining room volume. The living room springs out over the descending grade to the southeast, embracing the spectacular view. A steel truss structure frames the glass living room and dining room and acts as a counterpoint to the remaining volumes. Clad in stucco, metal, and vertical wood siding, they reflect the Futurist collages. The master bedroom suite is perched above the living room; garages are below the guest rooms. Paintings and sculpture are housed in the transparent living room wing while the more light sensitive works are displayed in the opaque bedroom and study areas. Recognizing the need for a central but private space, we separated the conical second-floor study from the activity in the rest of the house via a catwalk and stairs. Two floors below, under the kitchen/family room, a painting studio opens to a cloistered view of the garden.

The new house is a study in contrasts between traditional modernism and a new modernism. Rather than function fitting within geometric form, form springs from function.

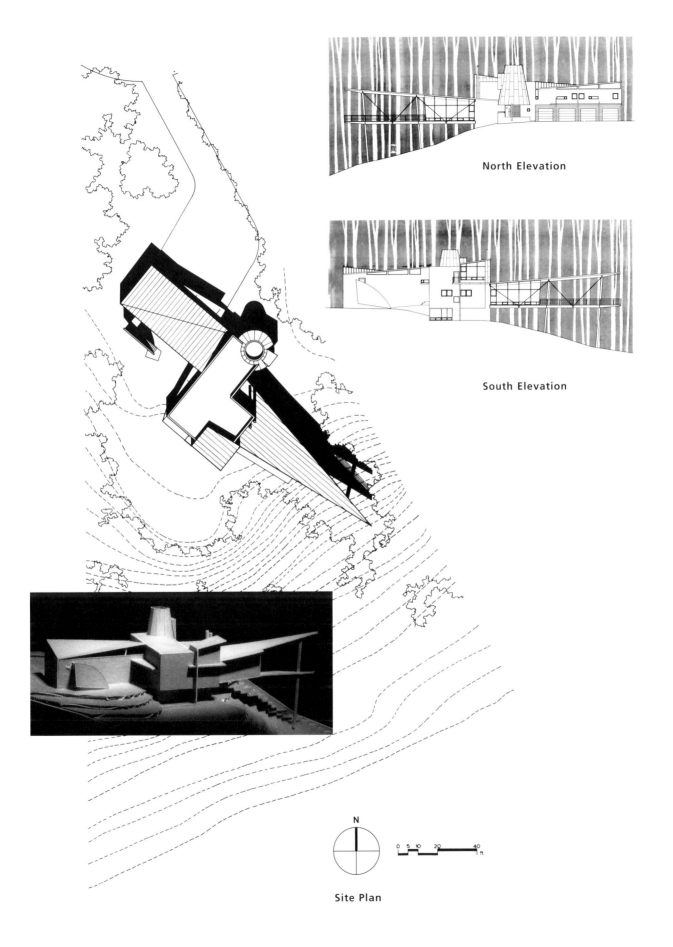

North Elevation

South Elevation

N

0 5 10   20   40
                    ft

Site Plan

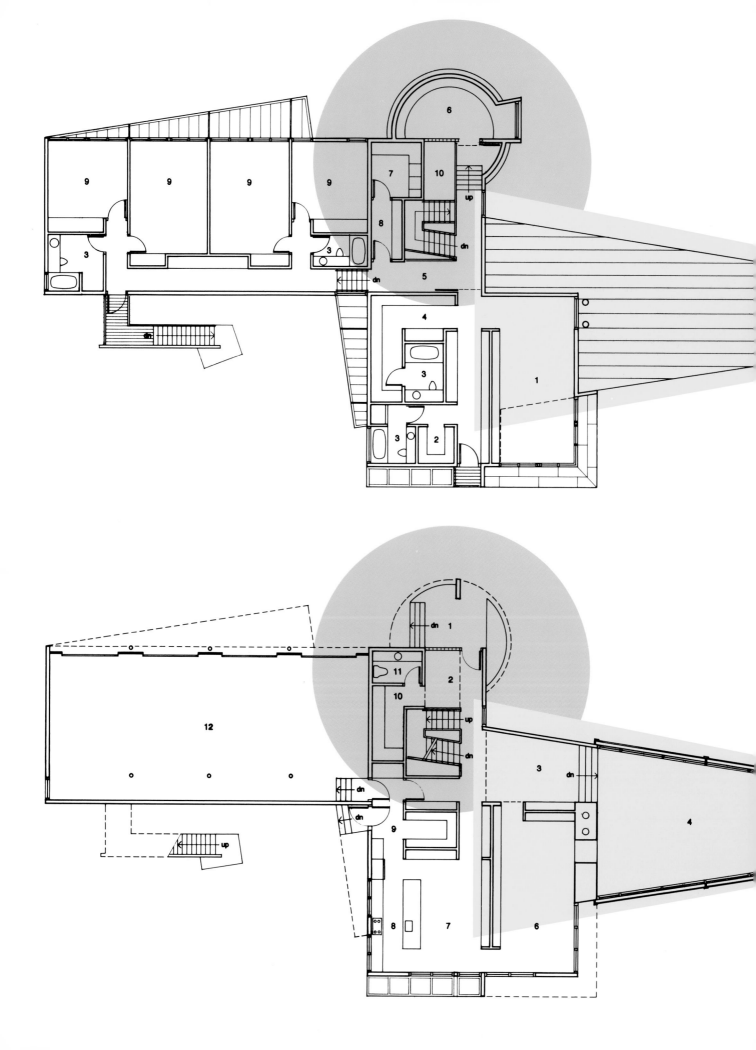

Second Floor Plan

1	Master Bedroom	6	Study
2	Closet	7	Laundry
3	Bathroom	8	Storage
4	Dressing Room	9	Bedroom
5	Stair Hall	10	Open to Below

*Canterbury
House*
1994
Watchung
NJ

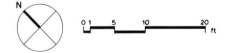

Ground Floor Plan

1	Portico	7	Family Room
2	Entry	8	Kitchen
3	Gallery	9	Pantry
4	Living Room	10	Storage
5	Deck	11	Lavatory
6	Dining Room	12	Garage

Clifty Creek
Elementary School
Columbus, Indiana 1994-

In the early 1940s, the architect search committee for the First Christian Church of Columbus, Indiana, with Nettie Sweeny Miller as a very active member, began a search for "the best architect in the country," as mandated by the committee. After interviewing many architects, they settled on Eliel Saarinen. During the design process, Mrs. Miller's son, J. Irwin Miller, befriended Saarinen's son, Eero, and Charles Eames, both of whom were working in Saarinen's office on the design of the new church. Through their friendship, Miller developed a great love of architecture.

Several years later, Columbus was growing rapidly and desperately in need of new schools, and Miller had become chairman of the Cummins Engine Company. Miller made a unique proposal to Columbus's school board: if they selected a "distinguished national architect" from a list of six names submitted to them, the Cummins Engine Foundation would pay the architectural fees for a new school. That offer subsequently was extended to the construction of all public schools and public buildings in Columbus. Consequently, Columbus now has buildings by both Eliel and Eero Saarinen, I.M. Pei, Robert Venturi, Richard Meier, Gwathmey Siegel, Edward Larrabee Barnes, Hardy Holzman Pfeiffer, and many other architects. To be part of the Cummins list is a great honor for a mature architect; we were amazed to become part of the list and to be commissioned for a project.

We were selected for additions to and renovations of the Clifty Creek Elementary School, designed in 1982 by Richard Meier. Eight classrooms, a sophisticated media retrieval system, teacher preparation rooms, and lavatories are to be added. Administrative offices and classrooms are to be renovated. Most difficult, but very important, the entire structure is to be retrofitted to meet the requirements of the Americans with Disabilities Act (ADA). The client, the Bartholomew Consolidated School Corporation, had a desire to maintain the integrity of Richard Meier's original design, and asked that our addition be seamless.

We have extended the primary axis of the school in both directions. Six classrooms stack west of the main classroom wing. A service link keeps the addition from appearing too massive. It also matches Meier's original setback at the juncture between classrooms and library and minimizes any difference in material shading between old and new. Two kindergartens are placed on the east end of the original building. The ADA-required elevator and corridors tuck neatly into the existing courtyard of the building, on existing foundations and beneath the existing overhanging roof.

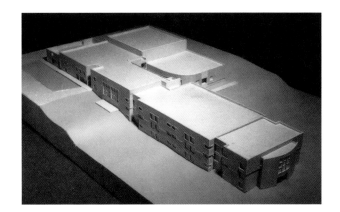

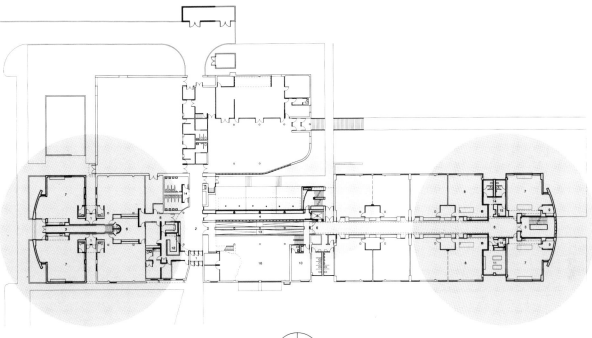

N

Second Floor Plan

1	Vestibule	9	Small Group Institution
2	Lobby	10	Media Retrieval Area
3	Stair Hall	11	Teachers' Preparatory Area
4	New Passage	12	Administrative Office
5	New Elevator	13	Existing Ramp
6	Public Corridor	14	Toilet
7	New Classroom	15	Janitor's Closet
8	Modified Classroom	16	Library

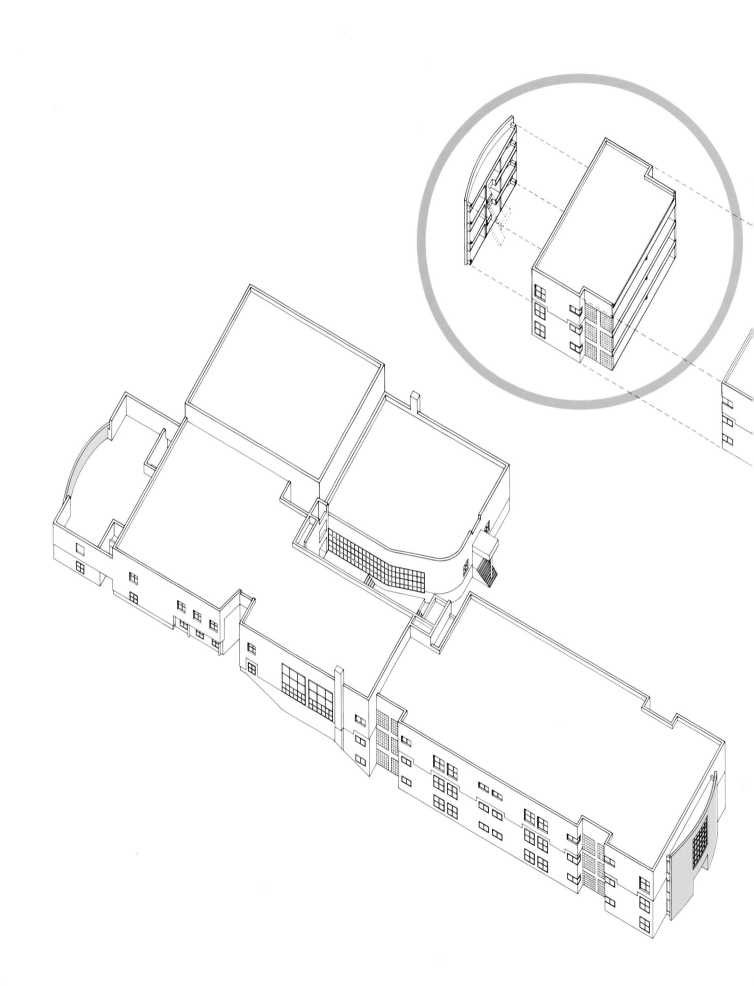

Clifty Creek
Elementary
School
1994
Columbus
IN

The Chimes Project
A GMHC
Volunteers Memorial
New York 1993

I depart as air, I shake my white locks at the runaway sun,
I effuse my flesh in eddies, and drift it in lacy jags. . . .

      Failing to fetch me at first keep encouraged,
      Missing me one place search another,
      I stop somewhere waiting for you.

      —Walt Whitman

At the epicenter of the AIDS epidemic in America is the Gay Men's Health Crisis (GMHC), the oldest and largest AIDS service organization in the country. With so much of the work and energy of GMHC coming from its volunteer force, the loss of each volunteer has a strong impact. A group of GMHC volunteers approached us and asked if we would design, for the roof of their building in New York, a memorial to GMHC volunteers who have died.

> From the start we knew that our design had to be a metaphor for many aspects of the AIDS crisis. Walls shaken from their bases represent the helter-skelter world in which the virus grows. East and west walls, oriented toward the rising and setting sun, slope outward, opening to the sky above. We chose aluminum primarily for its crystalline relationship to the central metaphor of the project but also for its seductive beauty and menacing danger. As a symbol of life, plants spring—in some ways miraculously—from metal panels. Carved niches create benches. The niche backs are copper, inscribed with the words of Walt Whitman.

Finally, and most important, within the four walls hang thousands of hand chimes. As friends visit the memorial, they can brush their hands across the chimes, setting free the musical notes of the harmonically tuned chimes. Each panel of chimes would be tuned harmonically to evoke a specific time, place, or event. From each chime, inscribed with the name of a GMHC volunteer lost to AIDS, a spirit sings.

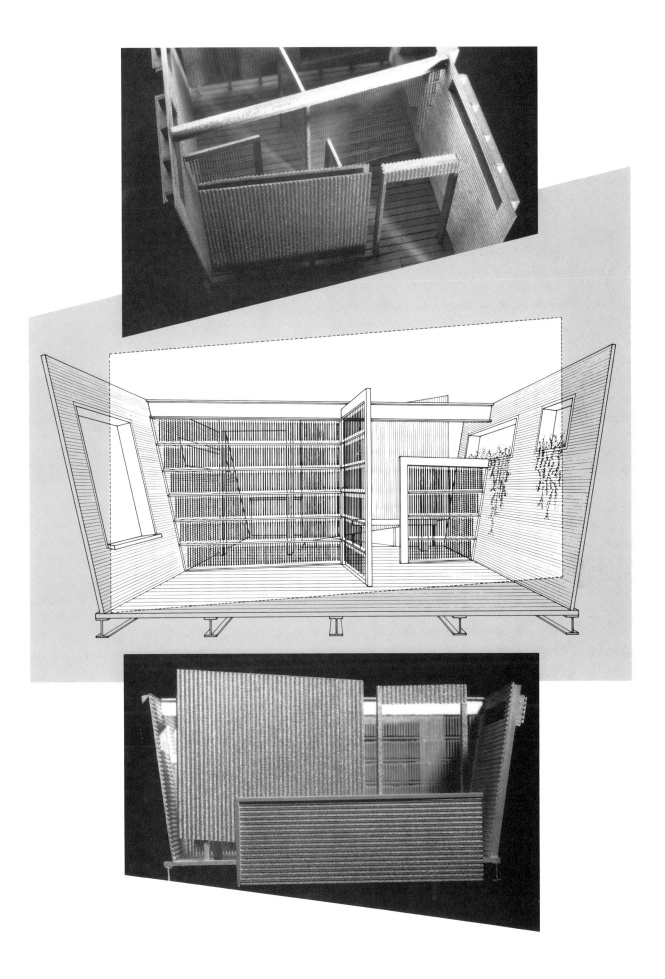

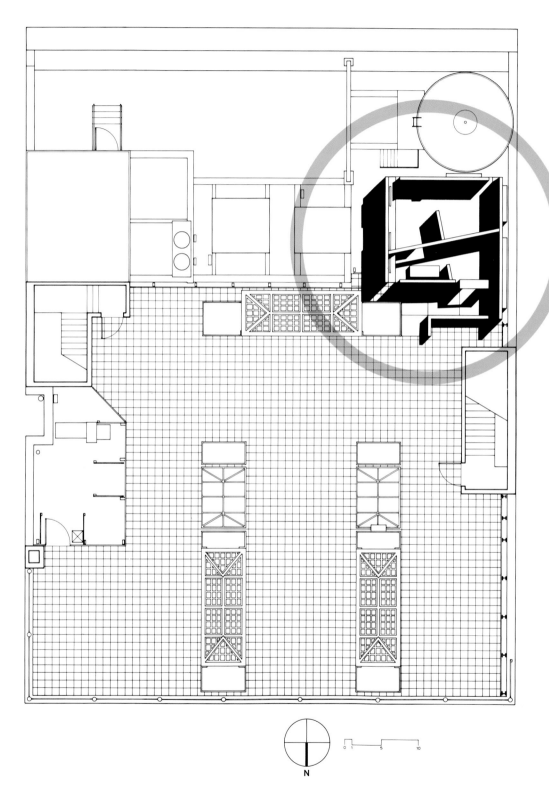

Roof Plan

GMHC
Volunteers
Memorial
1993
New York

Paul
Aferi
at

Peter
Stam
berg

Paul Aferiat attended Carnegie Mellon University, where he received his Bachelor of Architecture in 1975. He began his architectural training in the offices of Hardy Holzman Pfeiffer and Giorgio Cavalieri. He later worked in the office of Richard Meier & Partners Architects, on projects that included the Suarez Apartment, the Aye Simon Reading Room in the Guggenheim Museum, and the Hartford Seminary Foundation. In the offices of Gwathmey Siegel & Associates he was the associate in charge of the American Museum of the Moving Image in Astoria, New York, Westover School in Middlebury, Connecticut, and other commercial and residential projects.

Peter Stamberg attended Columbia College, Rhode Island School of Design, and The Architectural Association of London Graduate School of Architecture. He received his Bachelor of Fine Arts in 1972, Bachelor of Architecture in 1973, and AA Grad. Dipl. in 1975. He began his architectural training in the office of Davis Brody & Associates. He has written two books and has authored and been the subject of many magazine articles. His "Cardinal Dotts" chair is in the Contemporary Design Archive of the Cooper-Hewitt, National Design Museum in New York.

Their collaboration began in 1976, and Stamberg Aferiat Architecture was founded in 1989.

Bibliography

Wright Line Showroom
New York
1984

Dietsch, Deborah. "Media Is the Message." *Interiors*, December 1984, pp. 155–163.

Kraus Apartment
New York
1988

Bouchez, Hilde. "Kleurschock in de Upper East." *Belgian Weekend-Knack*, December 13, 1994, pp. 84–90.

Sueyoshi, Hiroki. "Upper East." *Casa Brutus* (Japan), Spring/ Summer cover, 1996, pp. 20–23.

Beach House Renovation
Seaview (Fire Island), New York
1988

Bates, Carol. "Beach House." *World Residential Design*, vol. 4, 1990, pp. 60–67.

"Bath Design." *Interior Design*, July 1992, p. 135.

Rus, Mayer. "A Modernist Makeover." *Interior Design*, November 1993, cover, pp. 140–145.

Kunstler, Deborah A. "Down by the Sea." *New York Newsday,* June 19, 1994, pp. 24–25.

Shumsky/Kronick Apartment
New York
1989

Bates, Carol. "Shumsky Kronick Apartment." *World Residential Design*, vol. 12, 1991, pp. 44–48.

Suarez Apartment
New York
1990

Anderson, Jean. "Kitchen Design What Works Best." *Food & Wine*, May 1996, pp. 101-103.

Rinaldi, Paolo. "Il Portale Giallo." *Casa Vogue*, February 1992, pp. 62–65.

Pittel, Christine. "Color! Color! Color!" *Elle Decor*, February/March 1992, cover, pp. 57–63.

Apartment for Tom and Linda Platt
New York
1990

Odoni, Giovanni. "Il Muro di Cartere." *Casa Vogue*, February 1992, pp. 66–69.

Waller, Kim. "Modern Means Joyful." *House Beautiful*, January 1993, pp. 58–63.

Waller, Kim, and Petra Carr. "United Colors of NY." *Privé*, April 1993, pp. 27–31.

Ward, Timothy J. "Breaking the Color Barrier." *Metropolitan Home*, May/June 1993, pp. 54–55, 70–71.

Kunstler, Deborah A. "A Fashion Statement." *New York Newsday, Home*, September 18, 1994, cover, pp. 30–32.

____ Copeland, Irene. "Day Glow." *Cosmopolitan*, January 1995, pp. 150–151.

Nelson/Sarna Apartment
New York
1991

____ Rus, Mayer. "Art + Life" *Out*, April 1995, pp. 124–125.

Stamberg Aferiat Loft
New York
1976 (Painted 1991)

Magnusson, Emanuela Frattini. "Loft a New York City." *Domus*, December 1993, pp. 48–51.

Bouchez, Hilde. "Kleur Bekenne." *Interieur Gids*, January 1994, pp. 14–27.

Balint, Juliana. "Couleur Locale." *Deutsch Elle*, April 1994, pp. 164–168.

Rinaldi, Paolo. "Un Gioco di Scatole." *Casa Vogue*, April 1994, pp. 146–153.

Balint, Juliana. "Her Bor 16 Skrigfarver og 2 Arkitekter." *Bo Bedre* (Denmark), August 1994, pp. 24–31.

Bouchez, Hilde. "Goed Amerikaans: Oude Stijlen en Felle Fleuren." *Eigen Huis + Interieur* (Belgium), December 1994, pp. 48–53.

Stern, Ellen. "Going with Matisse." *House Beautiful*, February 1995. pp. 102–105.

Aoki, Rei. "Stamberg Aferiat's House." *Modern Living*, September 1995, pp. 22–25.

Balint, Juliana. "Sechzehn Verschieden Farben Braucht Es Zum Bunten Glück." *Privé*, November 1995, pp. 26–32.

____ Girard, Jean-Yves. "Un Loft à Manhattan." *Elle Québec*, August 1996, pp. 100–103.

A Ceramic Collector's Apartment
New York
1993

____ Rus, Mayer. "Stamberg Aferiat on Fifth Avenue." *Interior Design*, March 1995, cover, pp. 87–91.

Long Island Children's Museum
Garden City, New York
1993

Story, David. "Scenes." *New York Magazine*, December 6, 1993, p. 40.

Balint, Juliana. "Museum für Kinder." *MD* (Germany), September 1994, pp. 58–61.

Rus, Mayer. "Art + Life." *Out*, April 1995, pp. 124–125.

Loukin, Andrea. "The Long Island Children's Museum." *Interior Design*, August 1995, pp. 70–73.

Stamberg Aferiat Lounge Seating for Knoll
New York
1994

Loukin, Andrea. "Seating." *Interior Design Market*, October 31, 1994, p. 31.

"Comfy." *Architectural Record*, May 1995, p. 47.

Ravaioli, Laura. "Design Made in USA and Europe." *Interni*, July-August 1995, p. 107.

Margolies, Jane. "Furniture." *House Beautiful*, May 1995, p. 40.

Balint, Juliana. "Sitzkisten in Baukasten." *MD*, November 1995, pp. 30–31.

Sycamore Creek House
Princeton, New Jersey
1994

"Natural Materials Used Naturally." *Architectural Record*, April 1995, p. 36.

Hoffman House Restoration and Additions
East Hampton, New York
1996

Kroloff, Reed. "Hoffman House Renovations." *Architecture*, February 1996. p. 40.

Clifty Creek Elementary School
Columbus, Indiana
1994–

Kroloff, Reed. "Clifty Creek Elementary School Additions." *Architecture*, February 1996, p. 41.

Furnish a Future
New York
1994

"Fantasy Chairs." *House Beautiful*, May 1995. pp. 46–47.

Photography Credits